BEFORE YOU WORK OUT, *EXERCISE*

BEFORE YOU WORK OUT, *EXERCISE*

40 Days of working it out, mentally and spiritually

Nadirah Aqueelah Shakir

iUniverse, Inc.
New York   Bloomington

BEFORE YOU WORK OUT, *EXERCISE*

40 Days of working it out, mentally and spiritually

Copyright 2010 © by Nadirah Aqueelah Shakir

iUniverse books may be ordered through booksellers or by contacting:

iUniverse
1663 Liberty Drive
Bloomington, IN 47403
www.iuniverse.com
1-800-Authors (1-800-288-4677)

ISBN: 978-1-4401-8050-7 (pbk)
ISBN: 978-1-4401-8051-4 (ebk)

Printed in the United States of America
iUniverse rev. date: 3/9/10

This book is dedicated to every woman that I've met on my fitness journey. Guiding you on your fitness quest has taken me on a journey of my own. Thank you for helping me to connect with my purpose.

Special thanks to Queen Sabine for helping me bring this project into fruition.

Fatih Abdul Malik and Vicki Ann Shakir I could never repay you for making health and fitness apart of my childhood.

Contents

Why I Wrote This Book

Here I am inviting you to take this journey with me. My intention is to help us become aware of the underlying issues that continuously keep us "working out" without ever reaching or maintaining our ultimate goal. I have faith that once we become aware we will began to exercise principles that not only give us the bodies we desire, but will give us all the good that God promised.

INTRODUCTION

Understanding My Lingo

You'll notice on this journey that I'll use **God** in one scenario and **Spirit** in another scenario. Let there be no discrepancy. God and Spirit are the same. You may notice that I call God my father and Spirit my mother. This will depend on the energy I feel at the time. I call that energy GOD or refer to it as "He" when my experience arouses a masculine energy in me. I call God by the name of *Spirit* or refer to it as "It" when my feminine energy is felt. All of us, men and women, possess both masculine and feminine energy, and we use them interchangeably depending on the situation. My point is I am not a polytheist. There is one power and one presence, and that is GOD. Because God uses us individuals to do its work, the expression of energy is not always the same.

Love is the idea of unity. God/Spirit is love. Imagine a husband and wife that gel together so harmoniously that they spread the power of love where ever they go. That idea of oneness expressing Its power is GOD/SPIRIT. We were raised to believe that God is a man, so we never considered that God expresses in feminine energy too. God has a feminine energy, but if you still want to think of It as only a man, that is fine. It doesn't make It any less powerful. I always refer back to the Bible when it says that God took Eve from the rib of Adam. I believe Eve was, in fact, Adam's feminine energy that was expressing itself.

Many refer to nature as '*Mother Nature.*' In my eyes, GOD is everything that is good and beautiful, so this includes nature. Whenever my intuitive nature kicks in, this is my time to rely on Spirit. I am feeling. My heart is leading me. When my heart leads, it feels like a sweet, gentle energy—similar to the feeling of my mother giving me a calming hug after a rough day. You've heard the phrase, "*Mother knows best?*" I believe whoever made up the phrase really meant to say, "Spirit knows best."

When I call on God, I am often formulating my thoughts, or organizing my intelligence for logic and analysis. Look at it this way. God is my mind. Spirit is my heart. In order for me to function at the absolute best of my ability, I need the two of them in sync.

Items for Departure

There are essentials we take on every journey. This journey is no different. The two essentials that you'll use on this journey almost every day are denials and affirmations. I like to refer to them as tools for consciousness, because when things gets a little shaky, I can always count on these tools to tighten things up. Don't worry! They won't take up space in your gym bag, because they're stored in your head and heart. Denials and Affirmations are your best bet for supplements. They are proven effective as it relates to weight loss and muscle growth. You won't find anything better on the market. You can trust me. I know all about *supplementing*.

Denials are used to erase negative thoughts. The use of denials takes away power from the things we do not want in our lives. In our case, denials are our fat burners. When using denials, it is important not to use them abruptly. This means you don't want to invest too much energy resisting something that you don't want to see. Energy is energy. Whatever we give our energy to, good or bad, will grow. This is why it is important to remain calm yet confident when denying and know that while *you* are denying, *God* is at work.

Affirmations work differently than denials. While denials erase and flush out, affirmations build and construct. However, you receive the best results when you use the two together. An affirmation is a proclamation of truth. We use affirmations to build on ideas that we would like to see more of in our lives. Affirmations are our protein and amino acids. They're essential for strength and healthy muscle.

There will be four other things you'll need on this journey. Those of you who are high tech will only need three. They are an open mind, a pure heart, a pad and pen. For those of you who like technology, you can use your lap top. These are the essentials that this journey requires. Anything else you want to bring along is up to you. My advice, *pack light.* Half the stuff we travel with we don't need any way. Oh yeah, as for your make up bag, leave it behind because on this journey we're going to *face up*! Besides, you'll need that extra space for something new!

Born into Fitness

When I was a little girl, my dad and mom used to work out at the gym. The gym had a day care, and we had to stay in it. **NO CHILDREN ALLOWED ON THE WORKOUT FLOOR!** *That was the rule.* It was written in big red and white letters, posted up high for all to see. I'll never forget it. Every time my parents told me they were going to the gym, I would get happy and jump in the car before they could get in. But when our dark blue 1976 Cutlass Supreme pulled into the crowded parking lot, my head hung low because I knew I had to go to the day care. Don't get me wrong. The day care was a lively and colorful place. Wall to wall, there were toys and games, and the day care attendant, Ms. Janet, was a saint. I just didn't want to be there. I wanted to be out on the workout floor exercising with the big people. So, one day, I came up with a plan.

There was only one bathroom in the day care. I waited until the bathroom was occupied and I told Ms. Janet that I had to go pee really bad. I stumped, danced like a snake, and tugged at my zipper until Ms. Janet insisted I go to the big people's bathroom. "Don't get into trouble," she warned as she put something around my neck. I guess it was some sort of pass, because when the big people at the front desk stopped me and saw the thing around my neck, they let me go. I went to the bathroom alright. I went to the bathroom, the pool, the aerobics room, the cardio machines, and the weight room. *I'll never forget the weight room.* There were big men in there, with big muscles; and my daddy was one of them. He was on the bench pumping some serious iron, but when he saw me, he rose up.

"What are you doing in here?" he asked in a stern voice with a sly smirk. I didn't know whether to smile or cry, but I figured with Daddy, I'd rather be safe than sorry. So I told the truth. *Well* kind of.

"I had to go pee," I said meekly. Now I was really about to pee in my pants. When Daddy smiled at me and took off his weight gloves to rub my head, I knew I was safe and suddenly the urge disappeared.

"Yeah, right. You just wanted to get your little hard-headed butt out of the daycare and in the big people area."

Daddy was right, but I didn't say anything at all. I just waited to see his next move. When he picked me up and sat me on the weight bench, chills of happiness ran up and down my little six year old body. When he handed me a weight, I showed all the teeth that were in my mouth, including the ones that were not there and the ones that were growing back. I must have done fifty curls with the weight Daddy gave me. He handed me another and said, "Don't waste your time curling light weights; *rep* something that is a little bit challenging." I was delighted. The wall-to-wall toys I left behind in the day care didn't even come close to being able to play in the big people area.

After thanking his workout partners for letting me interrupt their routine, Daddy made me wave good bye. They all smiled at me and squeezed my bicep like it had really grown in two minutes. Daddy walked me around the whole gym as if I hadn't seen it already. I just went along with it. We found Mommy by the leg machines. She was wearing some light pink tights, with a white and pink tank top. She never showed her stomach. She had her tights pulled all the way up over her belly button. Her hair was corn-rowed in tiny braids; but what she wore that stood out the most was a big Kool-Aid smile when she saw me. She was already in *squat* position, and she squatted even lower when she saw me to give me a big hug.

"How did you get out here?" she asked me with her arms still around my waist. I wasn't scared to tell Mommy the truth, plain and simple.

"I told Ms. Janet I had to pee really, really bad, so she would let me go to the big people toilet, and then I could see the whole gym."

Mommy looked up at Daddy. They smiled, rolled their eyes and shook their heads.

Just then, Ms. Janet stormed around the corner holding her very voluptuous and bouncing bosom in place. She was hysterically apologizing to Mommy and Daddy, but they assured her it was okay. Mommy assured me that she and Daddy would be a couple more minutes, and then we could go home. When I started to cry, Daddy called me Snaggletooth, which made me laugh. Then, he promised me he would race me five times when we got home, if I was good for Ms. Janet.

Ms. Janet took me back to the kiddy dungeon. On the way there, something happened. Ms. Janet got a chair and put it in front of the glass window, close enough to watch the big people exercise. She looked me square in the eyes and said, "Sit here and don't move. If you'll be good this time, I'll let you sit here next time." I sat there for what seemed like forever with my hands folded in my lap, showing all my teeth, the ones I had and did not have, and the ones that were growing back in. For the rest of my childhood, I sat there like a perfect angel. When I turned 16, Daddy and Mommy bought me my very own membership.

My Evolution in Fitness

Prior to my gym membership at age 16, I made the track team my freshman year. I became an athletic trainer my sophomore year. My senior year, I organized an all-girl aerobics class and recruited participants from school faculty and staff. My aerobics teacher entered me in the hall of fame for being a proactive female athlete outside of traditional sports. I drove my family crazy with the trampoline I had in my room. My sisters and brother couldn't watch TV in peace because I was running like Flo-Jo in the living room on the treadmill my grandma had given our family. I worried my Mom to death because I wasn't afraid to jog or ride my bike alone on the streets at 14 and 15. Fitness was definitely in my blood. Who would have thought that such a pure interest would have become tainted?

Like I said before, I've always worked out and I've always enjoyed it. I enjoyed the energy it gave me, the pep it put in my step, and the sense of harmony I felt when a nice run was complete. It's funny. Looking back, my intent for exercising was never to lose weight. I just wanted to feel like the big people looked who were jumping around in the step class. Although weight loss was not the reason for my exercising, my body did thank me for it in more ways than one. Weight loss was its obvious form of gratitude, and I was happy. The point is, at that time, I wasn't forcing anything. I was simply doing what I enjoyed without struggle and without strain.

I was about 23 when someone asked me if I was getting ready for a ***competition.*** Ignorant to what a competition was, I ignored the comment and continued my routine. By this time, I had already become a manager at the gym where Mom and Dad bought my membership. I was a personal trainer at another. While I had no idea what a competition was, I did know what being a model was, and that is what I wanted to be. While traditional modeling agencies told me that my thighs and butt were too big, one of my college professors told me I had *the look*. I found an agency that sponsored music video models. According to them, my hips and thighs were exactly what they were looking for. After one music video, I decided it wasn't for me. Shaking my booty in front of a camera wasn't exactly modeling. So I took the advice from the first agency, and started losing weight.

For years, I strived to get a model's body. My getaways on the treadmill were now torture sessions. Tendonitis, anxiety and palpitations were common now because I was overdosing **fat burners**. I was going to meet my goal by any means necessary. I wanted a piece of the American pie, but of course I was dieting, so there was no pie. No pies, no cookies, no bread, no rice, no sugar, no nuts, no fruits…. No food!

Anyway, I can't remember what I weighed, but I remember being so thin that Mom just looked at me. You know that look mothers give their children when they *know* their children are going in the wrong direction, but they don't want to fight about it.

"*Dira*," she said, "you look pretty and all, and your stomach is really flat, but are you sure you want to be *that* slim?"

Of course I wanted to be that slim. How else was I going to be in a fashion magazine?

Shaking my mother's comment off my back, I headed to my audition. I had never seen so many beautiful women in one place in all of my life. It was like a cultural melting pot in there. The one thing that everyone had in common was the fact that none of us had eaten the day before. Women were on the floor doing crunches and hip extensions. Being a newcomer, it was exciting for me just to watch. I was intrigued, nervous, and wanting to bail. Just as I grabbed my bag, one of the directors called my name. "*Nah-dray-ah Shroo-Key?*" I don't know how *Nadirah Shakir* looked anything like what that man called me, but I shimmied over anyway.

In the audition room, there were men everywhere. There was a camera man. A music man. The artist's main man. The door man. Finally, there was the man who told me to "look into the camera, say my name, where I'm from and dance." I did what *that man* said. The men all watched. Then the main man told me I was lovely, but I wouldn't get this part. He promised to call me if something else came through. In the meantime, I should lose some weight in my arms, gain some weight in my buttocks, and consider breast implants if I wanted to be successful in this industry.

Let's just say that I wanted to be successful, but I decided against that industry.

I continued to work out, but my workouts were different. Now, I needed the weights to be heavier. The treadmill couldn't go fast enough and I couldn't run long enough. I was now up to two and three workouts a day. My shorts couldn't get tight enough. If I gained a pound, I wore baggy clothes so no one would notice. My fat burners were losing their strength. I couldn't find the right diet. Maybe I should only eat grapefruits, or maybe I should try cabbage…maybe I needed to build my butt up like the man said at the video audition. In that case, I needed some egg whites. I was beginning to lose it.

That can happen when you take something so sacred and personal to you and expose it to all types of craziness. When you strip your original design down to nothing in an attempt to put someone else's make and model on it, you deprive yourself of the very thing God has promised you from the beginning: Self love.

You'll come up short when you measure something that can't be measured. You'll compromise your joy, peace, and freedom. Misery, frustration, and chaos become the prison in which you reside. The sick part is you're the one holding the key.

While I was at the checkout counter paying for my egg whites and grapefruit, the headline of a magazine caught my attention. "How would you like to become a fitness model?" *Like it? I'd love it!* If I was too heavy for video and fashion, maybe my figure was better suited for a fitness model and competitor. I added the magazine to my cart. The article said an applicant should have an athletic build, show **aestheticism**, and be symmetrically proportioned. That was me! All I needed was the stage!

After I told my mother, she gave me that look again. Her look didn't matter now because I was a full grown 23 and a half year old, who was living part-time with a well-established CEO, in his four-bedroom, two-car garage home, with the white-on-white baby grand piano, and the flat screen TV in the living room. I had a key. I didn't need her approval. I'd just ask my fiancé. I was sure he'd support me.

He didn't care for the idea either.

After all, he was a *butt man.* Anything compromising the butt was definitely a threat to the relationship. Still, he supported me. He woke up at 5 am to go to the track and drill me so that he could be at work by 7 am. The mornings he was too tired to wake up, I trained myself. I needed money for supplements. Most of my fiancé's money was tied up in real estate, so I broke my own bank. I spent my last $1,300 on supplements, registration fees, and suits. I still needed money for plane tickets, because, of course, the show was in New York.

It was like the modeling audition all over again. Only these girls had lived on chicken breast for weeks. It made them look rough and dry. I learned later that pigging out backstage on chocolate, sweet potatoes, and cheeseburgers was their way of *looking fuller*. Once again I was clueless, so I watched. These girls were so serious that they brought their own weights to the competition so that they could **pump up**. After they pumped up, they sprayed tanning lotion all over their hard bodies. The article said *toned,* but once again I was out of place, because I seemed to be too soft. They oiled their bodies with Pam cooking spray. Some girls taped their thousand-dollar suits to their bodies while others glued them on. Every time I walked, mine rode up. I took it as a lesson learned.

When they called my name, I mimicked those that had gone before me. I couldn't understand why some girls looked like they were sticking their butts out at the judges and smiling way too big. I learned later that was called **posing.** My posing score was the lowest. I placed a lousy sixth. There were only three spots available. Leaving the show, I promised myself that I would not allow myself to get involved in such mediocrity again. But, for some reason, I stopped by the judging panel to abuse myself with their opinions. "Next time, add a little more sex appeal," one said. "Take your hair off your face," said another. "Try bringing your shoulders out a little more; it will make your waist look smaller," said the woman with the silicone lips. As I walked away from the panel, the head judge gave me some friendly advice. "This is a competitive industry so you might want to tighten your hamstrings," he started, "and pay more attention to your gluteus maximus, if you're looking to make a career of this." I chuckled to myself, and vowed never to place myself under so much ridicule again.

Spirit had shown me in more ways than one that I was out of place. This was not holy ground, but I kept stepping onto it. Don't get me wrong. I have nothing against models or modeling. It's just that they are under such scrutiny. They are always in competition with themselves or someone else. It's a hard life to live. I began to study spiritual laws, and they assured me that life was not meant to be so hard. If something is mine, I shouldn't have to fight for it. God doesn't want us to fight. This doesn't mean I sit around while looking in the sky begging for my good to fall from it. It means that I *exercise* my right to accept all the good that has been promised to me. This means I trust, I know, I affirmatively pray, I direct my thinking, and I proceed as Spirit directs my path. There is no way that God would tell me to subject myself to that level of humiliation. My ego might have talked me into that, but not God.

You see, everything we experience, good or not so good, is a step in our spiritual unfoldment. Unfoldment is a natural process. It is a gradual uncovering. It also means to develop or grow. Notice I did not say spiritual *break through*, or spiritual *go get*. I said *un-fold*. That is a natural process which is in alignment with our purpose in life. Our purpose in life is to save our souls. We can only achieve this goal if God directs our path. Think about a rose. When you first see it, it is all closed up. After you cut an inch from the stem, and place it in a nice vase with some fresh water, it begins to open up. If you pour some fertilizer in the water, you had better watch out because that rose is going to open up so beautifully you can't help but tilt your head and smile at it. We are supposed to unfold like the rose, but we contaminate our fertile soil with all kinds of pollutants that stunt our spiritual growth.

We are given signs that let us know when we are in alignment with our purpose. These signs are our feelings. You will also know you are in alignment because the things that you need will be at your finger tips. People that can help you will be placed in your path. You might call them angels. They will ask for little or nothing at all, but their works will move mountains. These are just a few ways you will be able to identify when you are in alignment with your purpose.

The way you feel will be the surest sign of alignment. You should not feel frustrated, exhausted, sad, or overly anxious. You should flow like the river. Have you ever watched the easy flow of a river? Even though there are big rocks, limbs, branches, and sometimes animals in the path of the river, it does not stop its flow, nor does it change its flow. The flow is steady and easy. The river may be slow and easy, but it is steady. It never stops until it joins the sea. We need not fight our way through life. We should be like the river and flow until we reach our destination.

I Thought I Was Flowing

Now I had seven years of professional fitness under my belt. I spent three of those years in pursuit of everyone else's image of beauty, and all that I had gained was a whole lot of muscle. What I lost was money, time, and a sense of self. I can't remember when, but one morning I woke up and looked in the mirror, and I didn't recognize the young woman who stood before me. Frightened, I turned my back on the reflection. I sat in a corner in my room with my eyes closed trying to remember what I looked like before the bleached skin, bouncy Dominican wrap that fell under my chin, straight white teeth, and the symmetrically defined physique. It wasn't hard to remember, but hard to accept. Perhaps the pain associated with my past was too much to bear. Maybe I could not accept the fact that I had made all those changes in the name of beauty and still felt ugly.

It didn't matter now. What was done was done. I needed to focus on getting back in school and making some money. I needed to get *ME* together, because competing had definitely torn me apart. It took me about a week to find a job in fitness, three weeks to get hired, and four months to become the number one trainer in the district. I was top three in the company for almost an entire year. The job was easy. I knew fitness better than I knew myself. What I understood most was the *psychology* of the fitness industry. The majority of the people who came to join the gym were just like me. They were sick and tired, or sent in by their doctor because they were plain old sick. Then, there was the vain population who came in just to maintain and show off their cosmetic surgery. The psychological approach was the same—I make them feel good *temporarily*. My vice president and district manager could not understand why I didn't want to be a manager. I didn't want to manage people who sold dreams until I made my own come true. I still had some soul-searching to do before I even knew what my dreams were, let alone making them come true.

School was going great. My grade point average was 3.6, the highest it's ever been in college. After having dropped out so many times, it was hard to believe that I had less than a year before graduation. Work was great. Money flowed in; bills were paid off. I was even able to help Mom out around the house. I was on *my* path. I was flowing. I was *making* it happen, as my district manager used to say. Then, company policy shifted and my district manager started to post the training statistics in the break room. Month after month, it read, *Nadirah Shakir, Number one.* It was cool at first, especially with me being number one and all. When my co-workers' eyes started to turn green, things got a little uncomfortable. Co-workers, who I thought were my friends, started to take my leads and steal my guests. All of a sudden, my self-worth depended on how many guests I could *close* in one day. It was competition all over again. The authenticity of something I loved had been tainted, again. This time, it was easier to recognize. I called a meeting with my boss and district manager and told them how our new policy made me feel. Although they admitted to understanding my dilemma, they held the view that competition drove more business. They stuck with the plan, which meant my co-workers continued playing a war of cutthroat.

In every war, there are casualties. Then, you have those who have no physical signs of war, but they go home never realizing how the war affected them until they wake up screaming in the middle of the night. That's how it felt the last time we had sales competitions. This time I couldn't let it go that far.

I asked my manager for time off.

Daily, I sat quietly in the corner in my room. I was seeking guidance. So, I listened for the still, small voice of my intuition. Her words were clear. *The spirit of competition is still in you. If you truly want peace, go back to work and forget about being number one. Simply enjoy the work you do and ignore the daily club statistics. Help your fellow co-workers when you see them in need. If you want peace, try this.*

Before You Work Out, Exercise

I didn't know who this imposter was, telling me to *help* the people who were stealing from me to *make* money. This couldn't be Spirit. I closed my eyes again and I told Spirit to reveal herself and stop playing games with me. Then the phone rang. My eyes opened and so did my clenched fist. It was one of my clients informing me of an upcoming body competition. *Now that's God,* I thought, and because I felt good about it, that was my sign. He gave me all the information about the show. He even offered to help me with my nutrition. This time, the money was there, and because I requested time off from work, so was the time. The show was held in West Palm Beach so this meant no money wasted on air fare. I must be flowing.

I planned a 12-week nutrition and exercise regimen that was sure to get me to my desired results. Every day, I woke up before sunrise and headed to the gym like I planned. My nutrition plan was working like a charm. By week two, I had already lost six pounds. That wasn't fast enough. I needed my fat burners, and I mean the good stuff that you couldn't get your hands on in Miami. I knew every supplement shop in Florida, so I knew where to find some ephedrine. I worked out for three hours straight and didn't even feel it. Sometimes, I was a little nauseous and cranky, but my six-pack was coming in nicely, so I dealt with it.

I talked to all of my professors and told them that I would have to miss a couple of classes, because I was preparing for a show. That was fine with them just as long as I made up my assignments. I always did.

By week seven, I was feeling miserable. I was exhausted, cranky, and always cold. Every time I went outside in the heat, my skin broke out in a rash.

The body never lies. Things that we are afraid to admit, the body shouts out. Any discomfort in the body is a signal telling us to STOP or proceed with caution.

My tenth week, I met another competitor while working out. She complimented me on my body then offered to help me if I needed anything. I needed suits and she had them. She rented two of them to me for $100. Had I bought my own, I would have spent close to $1,500. I knew what bikini glue was now so no riding up for me. The show was mine! I renamed it the "*Nadirah Show.*" The little voice kept annoying me, whispering, *There is no competition in Spirit.* She kept asking me, *Are you a spiritual being or not?* I avoided Her question by justifying it as a show, not a competition. I didn't want to beat everyone else. I just wanted the judges to favor me. Favor me they did. The decision was unanimous. I was the first place winner in my class. I thought this meant that God was definitely on my side. Sure, someone stole my shoes back stage, but from what I understood, that was common at these events.

Immediately after the show, I went back to work. To my pleasant surprise, the employees who had started the game of cutthroat had either gotten fired or quit. My boss talked me into testing my managerial skills by managing the weekends. It went well. Those weekends were reportedly the best weekends that the company had seen in a long time.

Something still wasn't right. I couldn't put my finger on it. Even though things seemed great, there was something else going on. I couldn't understand it. *God* had let me win, so why was *He* making me feel guilty. Furthermore, where was this ferocious appetite coming from? I had put on all the weight I lost, plus more.

Since I couldn't put my finger on it, I continued to work. I couldn't afford to take more time off, so I had to deal with it. My client stopped by to inform me about another upcoming show. This time, I could receive my pro card. I would be recognized as a **professional figure competitor**. That meant I had to do everything I had already done *times two*. I had a lot riding on this show. First of all, it was a national qualifier, so I would be competing against some of the best physiques around the world. It would also be televised. There would be magazine coverage and a generous cash prize for the winner. The promoters would also pay for the winner's air fare, and send them to Las Vegas for the next show.

This was it! This was the big break I needed. I put my prayer request in at church along with a generous love offering. Maybe the prayer chaplains would pray a little harder for me. I did my affirmations and denials. I said I would eat fish and water for twelve weeks straight. Jesus ate fish; maybe if I ate fish like Jesus, He'd help me out. The word was out. All of my clients and family were purchasing their tickets. This year, I decided to buy my own suits. They arrived from California, Federal Express. Red, white, and blue, surely those were the colors of the American dream. I started taking my **fat burners** and **diuretics**, and eating my fish. Because the show was televised, I was advised to look as mainstream as possible. I invested in some authentic human hair.

One night after doing all this, I went home, and must have slept until noon. I woke up and decided I wasn't doing the show. When I told my mom, she just smiled, and continued braiding her hair.

There was no way I could torture myself like that again. I would have to reach the people in another way if that was *truly* my reason for competing. I did not need a panel of judges to assess my already beautifully made body. I surely did not want to go another day eating fish and water. I didn't know what I was going to do. The one thing I did know was that there was a message of holistic health that I wanted to get across, and this was a total contradiction of it. I consider myself a *truth student,* and my story was filled with secrets and lies. Although I am not perfect, I am striving for excellence. So I went back to the drawing board. This time, I would listen to the still, small voice, and not the loud overbearing ego.

When I truly listened this is what I heard: *Why are you still allowing your wounded ego to run your life? The pain from the past is no longer relevant unless you want it to be. Stop wasting precious energy trying to validate who you are. Invest your energies in the things you really love. You know what you truly want. Stop dancing around it and get to it. There is no better time than now. We've been talking about it since you were a little girl. Now is the time.*

I thought about what she said. All I could come up with was working out; but I was doing that already. So what else could it be? Then I remembered. I loved to write and I loved to teach. Before I ever discovered the athlete in me, I had discovered my voice. I remember how I used to fall asleep while reading and writing. My dad used to read to us at bedtime too. When I was in third grade I was on the *blue bird* team, for students who were advanced readers and writers. I remember I had so much energy in grade school my teachers got tired of putting me in the corner so they put me in charge of helping other students with their reading and writing assignments. If I finished my work first and there were no students to help, my teacher would shove me in a corner with a book and tell me to read until everyone was finished. That was just the punishment I was looking for. Spirit had led me to my dream. I promised myself that when I heard *Spirit*, I would obey.

You Don't Need to Beat Your Body Up to Shape it

The body is not just a piece of flesh that you can *pound* into a desired form. It is a fascinating unit with many complex functions designed by God to keep us alive. It is up to us to *live*. It is through the body that we get to express how we want to live. Life is the idea of activity, vitality, strength, and beauty. When the body is functioning properly, these attributes are expressed in magnitude. We can sit here all day and discuss the perfect mid-section, or building muscle for a desired body part. This is all relevant; but before you can really appreciate that, you must understand and respect the underlying work being put in to keep your body functioning properly.

Nothing beautiful can be expressed on the outside until it is functioning properly on the *inside*. I've trained many clients from the athlete, to the first timer. I've also trained clients with lupus, AIDS, and other types of diseases. Those clients had something else going on besides the physical aspect of training. In their minds, they were trying to fix, or strengthen a system that was not functioning properly underneath the skin. Understanding what was going on inside of them helped them to strive harder during their sessions. They trained with passion. They understood that each leg press, arm curl, or 10 minute interval on the treadmill could be changing the chemicals in their bodies to help them heal. For them, their sessions were not about ripped abs. They were about living or dying. It's funny because from that group of clients, the ones that stuck with it had a better quality of life.

Every day they trained and never missed a session. They also took their nutrition very seriously. They were under the assumption that they would somehow have a shorter life than the client who was training for a show. However, as they shifted their thoughts to more positive ones, spoke optimistically, and continued to exercise, their bodies responded positively as well. They exceeded their goal to just stay alive, and they actually began to *live* again, in some cases, better than before.

I'll never forget the client who told me she had AIDS. That was the first time that I knowingly had been face to face with a person with that disease. It was shocking. She was so vivacious. It was unreal for me to see someone that healthy with a disease. She was nothing like we see in our text books. She was what we saw on MTV, or in sports illustrated. After a couple months of training her, she invited me to her wedding/birthday party. My mouth dropped open. Then I slowly closed it and realized that because she understood what was going on inside her body, she nurtured herself inside out, both physically and mentally. She said she had been living with this condition for 8 years and she has never taken medication. I never saw her take as much as a vitamin. I saw her not too long ago, and both her and her uninfected husband live life to the fullest.

Because the body is a renewing organism, there's not too much that we have to do to it. Our real work is in our minds and hearts. My hope is for everyone living with diseased conditions to heal themselves by reconstructing their thoughts or, at least, living every day to the fullest.

On another note, I met a woman that just wanted to lose weight and tone up. During her consultation with me, she told me about a place where she bought most of her supplements. One of the supplements that she was taking had been created for people who had cancer. It was to help them keep toned muscles and their hair during the process of radiation and chemotherapy. She used it to build more muscle so she could burn more fat. Another supplement that she used was a natural hormone that was usually produced in the male body. She used that to suppress her estrogen levels so she would not become soft. She also had a doctor prescribe a medication for her so that she wouldn't get her period. When I asked her why, she said that her period got in the way of her workouts. She assured me it was reversible. After two sessions, I referred her to another trainer.

Right after letting her go, I began to question my own integrity. I was still using supplements. Not as complex as the ones she used, but I still used man-made supplements. Seeing how far she had gone to burn the last bit of fat, and get that last cut in her arm made me realize that if I didn't stop, I could be just like her, buying illegal drugs, and having my doctor prescribe drugs for me as if I were sick.

I wanted to stop, but I didn't want to gain weight. It was a slow process, but as time went on, I began to discard a lot of the chemically infused supplements and started trying healthy alternatives such as b-12, flax seed oil, branch chain amino acids, and things of that nature. Instantly my body began to change. I gained back a little weight. I had to breathe deeper on the treadmill to catch that second wind. My incredible endurance and stamina had suddenly disappeared. I realized that if I went back to those products, I would continue needing them to keep my body in shape. So I saved myself the headache and about $100.

After that, every time I wanted to go purchase a bottle of whatever, I'd sit and rock myself until the feeling went away. Then, I'd go to the gym and push myself to run the same 7 miles at the same pace I did while I was taking supplements. I found a treadmill right in front of the mirror at my gym. As I ran, I would ask myself, "Are you going to give up like a little baby because you don't have your fat burners, or are you going to remember who you are and get through this session strong?" Slowly it worked. Every day, I'd watch my knees take turns bending while my feet came down with such power and authority on that treadmill. I did the same thing in the weight room. I don't train that hard anymore. There's no need to. Once in a while for kicks I might go to the gym and really get down. I train for longevity now.

Our body's already have the muscle fibers, sensations, breath and power we need to be able to do anything we want it to do. We just have to tap into it. If you are using massive amounts of supplements (over the counter or illegal), ask yourself if you could achieve the same results without the supplements. If your answer is no, remember those things will always have control over you and if something is controlling you, you are not free. God wants you to be free.

If you said yes, that is good. It just means that the seed has been planted in fertile ground and you are ready to explore your true potential.

Understand I am not against all supplements. A supplement is a thing added to something else to enhance or complete it. My only hesitation with supplements is that most people become dependent before they explore what the body God has given them can do. I know you must believe it in your heart before you can see it. There is no need to beat yourself up. Love yourself, and be patient with yourself knowing all things work together for good.

If you are wondering what happened to the client that I referred to another trainer. She had a heart attack during one of her *own* training sessions. Since then, she has had a hysterectomy, and is recovering from reconstructive surgery after the doctors removed a cyst from her right breast. It's unfortunate because that was all a result of her not letting her body do what it was designed to do.

Comfort and Acceptance

Comfort is something that is attainable for everybody right where you are. To admit that you're comfortable does not mean that you are one hundred percent happy, and that you have it *all* going on. When you say that you're comfortable, you're just saying "I *chose* to make the *best* of the situation *now* while I am persistently working on what it is that I truly desire." *For faster results*, combine comfort with acceptance.

Acceptance is the ingredient that neutralizes anything "funky" you may have engraved in the tissues of your skin. When you practice acceptance, it allows you to release the sense of urgency that often makes you abrupt with yourself. When you accept, you don't block your peace of mind. Acceptance creates the space you desire to love yourself right where you are. This act of loving yourself brings your good to you faster.

Together, comfort and acceptance can create contentment, which can create happiness, which can create joy, which can create enthusiasm, which can create ecstasy, which can take you places not even American Airlines can get to.

We've all met that woman. You know the one who wasn't all that attractive, but for some reason, you felt ugly around her. Even on your best hair day, with your flawless makeup and designer clothes, she made you question your definition of beauty. She might have been sporting some jeans, a white t-shirt and a pair of sandals with her hair pulled back in a pony tail. You may have been wearing a Prada™ dress with some Baby Phat™ stilettos, fresh out of the hair and nail shop. For some reason, when you saw her, you felt as tall as an elf and heavier than an elephant. The one thing that she was wearing that you couldn't seem to find in any mall or department store was a radiant smile. The smile that she wore told you she had discovered something about herself that you yourself had not yet discovered about yourself, and wouldn't notice if you did.

Her body wasn't even all that; but her skin was radiant, and her eyes wore joy. She was all that and then some. Even though you silently admitted to yourself that she could afford to drop about fifteen pounds and take a Pilates class or two, you still wanted to be in her class to know what she was studying. So you walked up on her just a little. Wiggling and waggling in your Baby Phat™ heels, you get closer. Then you noticed the peace on her face, and the joy in her eyes. Because her persona is so inviting, you can't help but smile and greet her.

"Hello, how are you?"

"All is well, and to know that you and I are loved by the Lord makes it even better." As she walks away, a soft wind blows. The fragrance that she wears is sweet. It was one that you had tried on many times before. You liked it, but you did not purchase it. At the time, it was too strong for you.

Scratching the side of your freshly permed hair, and being careful not to smear your flawless French manicure, you remember the name of the fragrance. *Self-Acceptance*, you whisper to yourself. You remember that was the fragrance that didn't come off when you changed your clothes. It was the good stuff. It's the kind that when you wear it, everyone wants to embrace you.

Just a few years ago, I threw out all that watered down stuff, and stocked up. I have plenty left over. If you're feeling kind of funky I'll give you a spray. That should be enough to neutralize the *funk*, until you wash up, and change into some more suitable attire. *Don't be embarrassed by the funk. It happens when you exercise!*

Speaking of exercise, there's one that I want you to do. You can do it now, or you can do it before the first day of our journey. It's up to you. Whatever part of your body you're most uncomfortable exposing, uncover it. Take your hands, and gently caress it. Talk to it. Tell it how sorry you are for acting so snotty towards it. Let it know that you want to get to know it better by spending more time with it. Assure it that you're not trying to get rid of it. Instead, you want to help it become the best leg, tummy, arm, butt, whatever it can be. Whatever part of the body it is that you have issues with, be sure that you love it tender.

Truly Love Yourself

We readily admit that we love our partners, children, family members and friends. But for most of us, looking at ourselves and saying, "I love you with all your flaws." is a hard thing to do.

Self-love is very important. The relationship that you have with yourself paves the way for the relationships that you will build with others. If your love for yourself is based on how much money you made last year, then you'll build relationships with people who love you only if we oblige to their conditions. The minute you slip up, they'll take their love away. If you criticize your feelings and mistakes, then more than likely, you will build relationships with people who are very critical or downright verbally abusive. If you mistreat your body, by consuming mass amounts of alcohol, cigarettes, and unhealthy foods, then it is possible to attract people who will become physically abusive. What I've discovered is that people treat us the way we treat ourselves.

I know a lady who was verbally abused by her father as a child. She too is verbally abusive to her own children, but she is not aware. I also know a man whose parents used to beat him so badly that he bled. When he grew up, he abused himself with drugs and alcohol, and he too beat his children until they bled.

We must recognize the unloving behaviors we have towards ourselves because we don't want to perpetuate them. I'll admit that loving yourself isn't always easy. This is why getting comfortable enough to accept yourself is very important.

Four years ago, I was having a tough time loving myself; and boy did my relationships show it. After church one Sunday, I asked a prayer Chaplin to pray with me. After we prayed, she suggested that I meet with the assistant reverend of the church for counsel. Boy did that change my life. The reverend recommended that I read two books. They were both on forgiveness. He also recommended that I read first Corinthians from the bible everyday for thirty days.

In the books on forgiveness, I discovered that the person that I needed to forgive was me. We'll explore forgiveness in detail later on. Just remember this; it is impossible to love anyone that you cannot forgive. When you don't forgive, you're mentally and emotional incapacitated. You're also spiritually retarded. When you begin to put forgiveness into practice, that funky stuff begins to seep out of your pores and new vibrant cells begin to reconstruct.

Reading I Corinthians daily helped me identify what love should look like. My eyes were open wide now when someone declared those words to me. More importantly, it made me aware that while I often boasted about how much I loved myself, I really did not. With all the conditions I let others place on me, along with the conditions I placed on myself, how could I? Telling myself I'll love you more when you're a size five. I'll love you more when you get your braces off. I promise to really love you when you graduate from college. That's a short list. I placed so many conditions on myself I had to step back and honestly ask myself *did I ever* really love myself. Before I placed my conditions on me, I allowed others to place their conditions on me. Now was the time for me to accept myself no matter how rough-around-the-edges I was. Slowly but surely, the conditions began to fall away. I began to love myself so much that, miraculously, the voices of those around me were silenced. The people who placed conditions on their love were people whose love I did not want. I began to cherish myself in every stage of my development. Soon, the only voice I heard was my own, and boy, did it sound sweet.

I want to share this with you. Most of you are probably familiar with I Corinthians. If you're anything like me, the day the preacher introduced it to me was the first time I had ever read it. Anytime you need to remember what love is, turn to this page. It will bring you back to yourself, and neutralize any and everything that tries to disguise itself as love.

"Love is PATIENT; Love is Kind. Love is not jealous or boastful; it is not arrogant or rude. Love does not insist on its own way; it is not irritable or resentful; it does not rejoice at wrong but rejoices in the right. Loves bears all things, believe all things, hopes all things, endures all things, Love is a __patient__ heart. Love never ends."

As I read those words over and over to myself daily, they began to penetrate my mind and my heart. As they settled in my heart, it became clear to me that God *is* LOVE, and because we are made in God's image and in His likeness, it is our inherent nature and our spiritual duty to be expressions of LOVE, the most powerful force in the Universe.

In those times when we are feeling envious, prideful, conceited, resentful, condemning, doubtful, defeated, and anxious we must reconnect and revisit our Father/Mother God, and claim the truth of our being. We must proclaim gently focusing our attention on our hearts. "I am patient. I am kind. I am meek but confidant. I have strength and endurance. I am patient with myself and others. I am a perfect expression of God. I AM LOVE.

Let's define the word gene. The dictionary defines a gene as *"a unit of heredity which is transferred from parent to offspring and determines some characteristics of the offspring."* In case you didn't know, a unit is complete already, but it is also able to form an individual component of a larger whole. You are a unit, and so am I. Individually, we are already perfect, whole and complete. However the one source and the one power in this Universe *which is* God urges us to form bonds with other souls to fulfill God's master plan.

Let's go back to genes and the transfer of them from parent to child. If I asked you to identify my parents, and you said, "Vicki and Fatih Shakir," you would be correct, *partially.* Those are my biological parents. My *real* parents, Father/Mother God don't have physical bodies. So they carefully selected Fatih and Vicki Shakir for me based on the needs of my soul so that I could carry out my assignment here on Planet Earth. I thank God for my parents I love them dearly.

We call ourselves children of God all the time because it sounds cute. The truth is we really are God's children. Now ask yourself this. *Can God get sick?* Is *God addicted to food? Is God poor? Does God curse people out? Surely not.* I am a child of God therefore I have Gods' genes, and so do you. If you don't believe that use this journey to find and connect to your true parents. Through meditation and prayer, you can contact your Father God and the Holy Spirit. When you've made that connection you'll discover that *you,* my beloved child of the most high God are royalty, and this Universe is your Kingdom.

We've been conditioned to believe what we see, and we have to break this habit. You can start by claiming the things you want by focusing on them and speaking on them. You can also ignore what you don't want more of. Since I learned that I have the power to do that, I started claiming and ignoring things left and right.

For example: I have a grandmother who is 76 years old. She has never been sick a day in her life. She doesn't have a wrinkle on her face. She can out dance me, and out walk me if I let her. She eats balanced meals, drinks lots of water, and has a personal relationship with God. In the romance department, let's just say when we go out, guys my age are asking her for her phone number. I claim those genes all day long. Every time I see her, I tell her how beautiful she looks. I tell her to rub some of her youth off on me. She always does. She doesn't sit around and complain and feel sorry for herself. She gets up and she does whatever she wants to do. You know, she never learned to drive, but because her spirit is so good she always has a ride. The days when she doesn't, she has two feet, and a bus pass. I claim that!

I have aunts who make the teenagers in our family look like *they're* in their thirties. I claim that too! I have a mother with such a humble loving spirit; she can make an ice cold drug dealer have a change of heart. I have a father whose smile can brighten up the city after a major power outage. I claim all of that and whatever else that is positive that my biological family has to give! What I don't want, I politely tell them they can keep it, and I keep moving without a second thought of it. I advise you to do the same.

Find a Purpose that's Good Enough

When you work in fitness, there are many reasons people want to get in shape. Very few stand the test of time. I want you to understand that I approach fitness holistically. Toning your inner thighs will get you nowhere if you can't think right. I once trained a beautiful client, Monica. She came to me wanting to lose 5 pounds and tone up her butt. She said she didn't care how much it cost. She took pride in telling me she was a stripper and could pay me five hundred dollars cash every week. That was cool with me. At twenty three years old, the furthest I had gotten into spirituality was near the end of Iyanla Vanzant's book, *Value in the Valley*.

Anyway, I looked at the young woman and wondered what else I could possibly do to develop her body, which was already perfect. When I say banging, she was *banging* like an African drummer boy letting the tribe know that a white man had just jumped off a boat. She had long blonde hair that stop at her very lower back. Her gray/hazel eyes complimented a very wicked eye brow arch that made her French vanilla face look like a seductive Cinderella. She had to be all of 5'3" at an even 120 pounds, which was already very toned. Yes, she did have a very perky *breast job*, which she told me was her third one because of past complications, which included child birth, silicon leakage, and a fight that she had gotten into at a club when the girl hit her in her breast with a beer bottle. Her waist was so small I could wrap both my hands around it and *still* have space; and the butt she wanted to tone was already toned enough.

Monica had a wedding ring that was so thick, it came all the way up to the knuckle of her ring finger. It was platinum on the back, and tiny diamonds all over the front. She told me 5 karats sat smack dab in the middle of her small treasure. Her hair was always nice, with lighter shades of her original blonde locks. Her clothing was always very fashionable, especially for gym attire. Nothing less than Nike®, Adidas®, and the latest Brazilian-cut, two-piece outfits. Sometimes I thought she wore some of her stripper outfits to the gym. These days you really can't tell. Her sneakers were always new; and all of that covered her already athletic frame.

I did my job. Monica wanted to tighten up her already tight butt, fine. She wanted to lose another 5 pounds and fade away, great. She always paid on time, every week, in full. I was cool with that, and plus she didn't mind if I worked out with her, which gave me my money's' worth and freed up time so I can get home and study. She was already athletic so she didn't slow my workout groove. Everything I did, it took her a set or two to match my intensity. Once we got in the flow, we were good to go. I spotted her. She spotted me. I racked her weight. She racked mine. We became friends.

Monica wanted to spend more time with me outside of training. I didn't have much time because I had school work. Besides that, I had just enrolled in some classes at my church. For some reason, my fiancé didn't like the idea of us spending time together outside of training. Since I didn't have time to socialize with her outside of training, she would call and we would talk. She said that I was mature for my age, and easy to talk to. I was.

One day, she came to the session with blood shot red eyes. She looked like she was carrying a *tad* bit more weight around the mid section. I ignored what I saw and began loading the weight to start our leg routine. "I don't want to train today," she said. "I just want to talk." Good, I thought. I was starving. I had rushed there to meet her after class. I hadn't eaten since egg whites and O. J. at 5:00 am. We sat by the smoothie bar and I had a protein shake and a tuna wrap that she paid for. I listened to her talk. She was too stressed to eat.

"I hate my life. All I want to do is be happy. Why can't I be happy? I need to get away. I think I'm going to go live with my sister in Virginia. I think I want a divorce. We're not really married anyway; he just bought me the ring. I don't want to be a stripper anymore. Maybe I should be a trainer like you. Don't ever have any kids. It's going to be $4,000 for another surgery. Maybe I should get a butt implant too…" She went on and on, which was good because by the time she finished talking, my food had already started to digest.

I liked Monica. I thought she was too young, too attractive, and had too much going for her to be in the position that she was in. Monica was clearly about money. So, to tell her the obvious and have her actually listen was farfetched. I didn't know what to tell her. So I started off with just that.

I wiped the tuna from the cracks of my lips and said, "Monica, I don't know what to tell you. The only thing that I can say is you have your whole life ahead of you. Not to mention you have three beautiful little girls who are watching you and depending on you. You need to do better for yourself."

"I know," she agreed now with the tears rolling down, like we were not in a public place. I didn't want to bust her bubble but I had to say what I felt. If she didn't want to train with me anymore, who cares?

"You need to stop stripping. Your body is not the only thing you have going for yourself. Didn't you tell me you went out for the police academy?"

"Yeah."

"What's up with that? Why don't you try that instead? They are both dangerous jobs, except one has a sense of honor to go with it." She agreed and said she would stop stripping. She told me that she had just passed her lie detector test and was waiting for some other part of the test to come back. We didn't train that day. I walked her outside to her husband's two-day-old Cadillac Escalade(tm) with spinning rims. Before I knew it, I had reached in my gym bag and pulled out my copy of Iyanla Vanzant's *Value in the Valley*.

"Here, Monica. Read this. It's seems as if it's written for black women, but we're all the same. Since you're going on vacation you can start reading it on the plane. I'll see you when you get back". We hugged tight hugs, and I help her strap her girls in their seat belts and car seats. I went back in to get a quick work out. Months past and I hadn't heard from her. Last I heard, her husband had beaten her up in a strip club after he found her giving a little too much service to one of her clients.

I learned a lot from Monica. I learned that looks didn't mean anything if you didn't know your worth. No matter how much money you have, you simply cannot buy your way out of misery. Misery, like freedom is a state of mind; and if you don't know how to use your mind, you're likely to stay in that state forever. These were good lessons for me at the time. In my early twenties, on the outside, Monica represented everything I wanted to be. I needed her to come into my life when she did.

I'm not saying don't make self improvements, but find a reason, one that will hold true after your body is cremated or sealed in a pine box. Last but not least, I learned never give away a gift that was given to you to someone who is not ready. Weeks later, I spent a whole 15 dollars at Barnes and Nobles replacing the book that my aunt had given to me.

A couple weeks later a new client had come and took Monica's slot. She was 5'6 and carried a very pudgy 176 lbs. She could use my services, I thought. Since she only had about 20 pounds to lose, I knew it wouldn't take long if she trained with me at least 3 times a week. Kara was the total opposite of Monica. She was a tad bit on the chubby side, thick legs, heavy buttocks, wide waist, and small arms. Her explanation for training with me though had absolutely nothing to do her body.

"I need more energy," she said, "My fiancé and I want to start a family so I want get in shape before I conceive." *All rightly then* I thought, let's get it done! Whatever you want, I got it! Sign your name on the dotted line and let the games began.

Kara was always on time. She usually sat at the smoothie bar before I got there. She was a school teacher so she came right to the gym after work, changed clothes, warmed up and waited for me.

"I'm not going to be able to train 3 times a week like you suggested. My fiancé and I are just settling in our new home and we still have to furnish it; and plus you know what's going to be our biggest expense." She looked at me and rubbed her chubby stomach and smiled. Kara *was* chubby, but she was cute. She had a jaw length bob that matched the color of her dark brown eyes, and fell nicely over her pale skin. She was always so bubbly like she already received the energy that she was *supposedly* coming to get.

"Alright, we'll start with two, but I'm going to require that you take a body-sculpting class for the extra day of weight training that we'll miss together and do an extra day of light cardio as well. I need to have you here at least 4 days a week if we're going to reach our goal." She shook her head in quick agreement, wrote the check and told me she wanted to start with her abs since that's where the baby would be staying for nine months.

That was no biggie. After the session was over, she confided in me that the doctors had told her and her husband that they would never be able to have children. She said she refused to believe that and was going to get pregnant by the end of this year and I was to help. I'm thinking to myself, *I am a personal trainer. I help sculpt the body, and help you lose or gain the weight. All of this about helping you get pregnant, you need to talk to your husband about that. If that doesn't work, you can try a surrogate mother or go to the good old fashion sperm bank.*

Kara said she didn't know if she or her husband was responsible for the infertility. She didn't care. She told the doctor to withhold that information. She was going to do what *she* needed to do before she went pointing the finger and adding insult to injury. Kara said she had never been unhappy to the point of depression about her weight gain but admitted to wanting to lose a couple of pounds to be healthy. Now that she had affirmed that her baby was on the way, she had the perfect reason to start and stick with it. She admitted that she did want her baby to receive the benefits of living a healthy life and living in a healthy mommy for nine months.

Kara and I trained for 5 months. She lost 15 pounds, and gained 6 pounds of muscle. She lost 4 inches off her waist and gained it all back plus more when her training was interrupted do to her pregnancy and delivery of her healthy baby boy. Kara sent a bouquet of roses and a thank you card to my gym with a picture of her baby boy.

Sixteen weeks later both Kara and her husband returned to the gym, and requested me as their trainer. Kara taught me one of life's biggest lessons. Attitude is everything! Right thoughts and right feeling produce the most beautiful results.

Now, before you go lacing up your sneakers, ask yourself, "Why am I taking this journey?" State your intention, and be sure your purpose is a valid one. An intention or purpose is very important because when the roads get rough, you are able to continue on. If your reason is to fit into that black dress, that might get you started, but it *may not* be a strong enough reason to keep your focus. If you lose the weight for that reason, you're more than likely to gain it back after you have worn the dress. Before you begin this journey, it may be a good idea to write down your intention, and place it somewhere visible.

God's Gift to You is Your Body

Someone might wonder why I am so concerned with the body if it's really all about self-acceptance and love. Some may even say it is a contradiction to place so much attention on the body if the mind does all the work. Understanding why you may think this way, I ask that you suspend your current beliefs and allow yourself the opportunity to expand your awareness.

Let me ask you this. If I came up to you and struck up a conversation with you but you couldn't see me, would you talk back to me, or would you ignore me and start to walk a little faster? I imagine most of us would question our sanity and start to run. I believe this is what God knew when He created Abraham, Jesus, Muhammad, Buddha, and all of the other great messengers. I believe God said, "Fellahs, I better put some flesh on you if I want to get my point across, otherwise folks won't listen."

The body is only flesh that God put on us, so that we can relate to each other, without admitting ourselves to a psychiatric ward. While it is *only* flesh, God thought it essential enough to add it to creation; therefore we need to honor it.

Understanding that having a relationship with God and loving and accepting yourself are crucial for personal development, you should also take into consideration that man and woman are complete and whole when he or she unifies mind, *body*, and spirit. Only then can the ultimate *demonstration* be made. We live in a physical world. Surely, this was not a mistake of the Lord *you* declare as *All-Powerful, and All Knowing*.

I've met several women who call themselves spiritual. I've also met people who are very religious. What I've found with these people is that the majority of them suffer from one illness or another. When I ask them to consider incorporating positive thinking, health, and fitness with their biblical studies and prayer, or with their spiritual studies and meditation, they often shake their head at me in disagreement, and then hand me some dogmatic religious *view* about why they should not exercise.

Believe it or not, many women are still allowing themselves to be oppressed by husbands and the ludicrous idea that a woman should not work out. For some reason, it is in their consciousness that a woman who strengthens her body is evil. As a result, they suffer in silence. They hide obesity, high blood pressure, diabetes, and other debilitating diseases under sanctified, long garments. It is crucial that we explore what the body really is and *God's* relation to it.

God has created us perfectly. In fact, we are made in His image and likeness. We are the ones who reconstruct the perfect original design that we were already blessed with. If we smoke, we reconstruct our lungs for cancer. If we eat foods that are high in fat, we build cells that carry more adipose tissue. If we listen to vulgar music, we begin to think in a vulgar manner about ourselves and our surroundings.

On a more positive note, if we eat fresh fruits and vegetables, we maintain the health that was already given to us. If we exercise, we strengthen our bones, joints, and muscles. When we spend time in prayer and meditation, we become consciously connected to Spirit, and we continue to live life *holistically*, the way it was intended.

What Are You Conscious Of

The consciousness is the sense of awareness and knowing. Our consciousness is the accumulation of events ideas, perceptions, and conditions. All of these *highly* affect our current state. Everything that we are aware of, *mind*, *body*, and *soul* make up our consciousness. The consciousness is in no way limited to what is intelligent or what can be logically reasoned or proven. Nor is it stagnated by the five physical senses. Consciousness includes a sense of awareness that cannot be seen. Intuition, premonition, or whatever you wish to name it, they all play key roles in conscious development.

What we are conscious of now affects our state of being. This is why we must focus on the things that will bring us closer to the desires of our heart. If you look at yourself in the mirror right now, your eyes may not like what they see. I ask that you try again, this time closing your eyes and imagining the body that you wish to bring into fruition. After you have done that, open your eyes again, look at your body, and you will notice a difference. This imaginary process will invoke feelings of hope and contentment because you are now aware of the fact that the body that you have now is not one that you have to keep if you don't want to. When you began to think right and feel right about your body, it is then that the body you wish to express will materialize.

Our consciousness is the key to building the lives that we desire for ourselves. Think of your consciousness as a computer that has a lot of data already stored. Some data you could have stored. Some data belongs to a couple of your classmates that you let use your computer. Your mom or dad could still have some of their old files stored there. There are old programs that have been installed that you no longer use. There's just a lot going on. After a while, the computer contracts a virus. Now you have to set up an anti-virus protection program. The program is designed to guard the system for any data coming through that might crash your system, or cause another virus. It is advised that before you install this anti-virus system, you clean out old data and programs that you can no longer use. After a while, your system operates sharper and faster.

You should apply the same concept to your mind. Set up a protection for your consciousness. Delete files that are old and outdated. Carefully check programs that belong to others, and see if you can use the information they installed, and if not, get rid of it. This will be paramount for building and expanding your new consciousness. Now, we're prepared to start the journey!

The Significance of 40

The prescribed time for this journey is forty days, and no, it's not just because Jesus spent 40 days in the wilderness. Although this may be a wild journey for some, it takes forty days to break an old habit and learn a new one. My belief is that the mind and the body work together. While the mind may want to forget a habit, the body still has sensations that make it physiologically attached. This makes negating the behavior a challenge. With consistent behavior during forty days, both of them will come to an agreement to either let go of something or start something new.

As it relates to physical fitness, almost all major changes of the body are made within the first 30 days. So, why not thirty? I chose 40 instead of thirty because this is a journey. That means, there will be some ups and downs, and just because you aren't conditioned for it, doesn't mean you have to stay behind. It'll be times like these that you'll need the extra rest.

Breaking down the 40 Days

The layout of our journey will be simple. 40 days will be broken up into 10 day increments. Every 10 days will represent one of the four seasons. For example, ten days will be spent in winter. Ten days will be spent in spring. Ten days will be spent in the summer, and we will be rejoicing, after our ten days in the beautiful fall. Got it? Good!

During each season, we will be working with a spiritual or universal law. We will also be working with a denial as well as an affirmation. Daily, there will be a word used to help us put these spiritual laws and truths to work. This is for our spiritual exercise. On this journey, all spiritual exercises must be done first. When we're done exercising spiritually and mentally, we'll get to what most of you really want to do, work out. So, are you ready?

Let's do this!

Spending time in each season will help you make the necessary adjustments you need in order to grow. Growth simply means to change and transform. Just like there are stages of growth in both spiritual and mental development, the same is true for the physical. God knew undergoing change and transformation would yield us a better life. He made it evident for us by giving us the four seasons. During the four seasons, we learn to adapt when we need to adapt, and change when we need to change.

Seasonal Meal Plans

Winter. For the first ten days, eat fruit and vegetables. That includes salads, but *without* the cheese, bacon, crotons, or other dairy products.

Spring. Your second ten days, you'll be eating less fruit than in the beginning. Consume veggies with every meal and fish of any kind. At this point you can include all of the fats that are in oil form.

Summer. Now, slowly add dairy products into your diet. Yogurt first, and then proceed with the other dairy items. You can also add chicken, turkey, and eggs in at this time, along with a few nuts.

Fall. You can enjoy anything from the last 3 seasons while still enjoying a vegetable with every meal, except breakfast.

If you feel that your body can benefit if you eat the foods in winter, spring, summer, or fall longer than the prescribed length of time, do so. Be sure to consume at least half a gallon of water a day. A whole gallon is excellent.

Spending Time in Your Winter

I love the winter. I live in Miami, Florida, so we get *very nice* winters. In any event, I still love it. I've experienced it briefly in travel in other locations of the world, but winter remains the same where ever I go. It might be snowing, just a little frosty, or Mother Nature may throw us some of her sharp ice cold winds. Winter feels good to me.

It represents a time of calmness. In the winter, there's very little movement. Perhaps Mother Nature is in meditation seeking God's counsel on exactly how to prepare for the rest of the year. The days in winter are shorter and nights are longer. When spring approaches the days get longer; but, *in the beginning,* the nights rule. At this time, all around the world, liquids turn into solids. Bodies of water such as rivers and ponds freeze over the top, but beneath the ice, there is still life.

Have you ever stepped outside on a nice winter day? If you haven't, try it sometimes. Take a jacket, go out and just listen. It likes meditation in slow motion. Nature is silent. There are no birds chirping. There are hardly any dogs barking. Children are inside because their mothers don't want them to catch a cold. The skies are still and there is peace all around.

This is an excellent time for thinking. Some may call it death. I call it the beginning, preparation time, a time for waiting. Not too many people like to wait. You see the seed was planted long ago, since the beginning of creation. Now in the quiet and the stillness, it is gathering its strength to manifest.

This concept reminds me of the conception. When a man and woman make love, if life wants to express itself, no condom or birth control pill can stop it. This is true in nature. In this season, farmers seem to struggle to produce crop. On the surface, it appears as if nothing is going on. The human being is trained to see only with the eye, so they panic when their seeming good does not show up immediately. However, the one who has expanded his consciousness knows in mind and heart that something greater is on its way.

For some of you, the first ten days may be cold. Things may seem as if they are not moving. They are; so weather it. When you feel like things are moving at a snail's pace, keep in mind that, inside of you, something else is going on. The sooner you realize that the better. One day, you'll put on a dress, and you'll realize that something has happened, that your eyes could not possibly catch. Be patient with yourself. A metamorphosis is taking place. Here comes your Spring.

Showing off in Your Spring

The beauty of Spring reminds me of a room full of multi-cultured women of all shapes and sizes, with different hairdos, and artsy attire designed for them. Even though I love Winter, who could deny Spring? She has light rains with the sun still shinning through. She has rainbows that add allure and color. Every flower you could imagine is decorating the landscape. The rivers are back in the flow and everything on the ground seems ripe and ready to eat. All the plants, crops and veggies are lush. During this time, love is lavishly expressed, and children love to play.

In spring, the weather is not too hot and not too cold. The temperature is just right. Summertime lovers can share in the consciousness that Spring is a good thing. During Winter, you endured most of the hardships to make the way for free flowing Spring. Spring is a time for new growth and rejuvenation. We all need a little bit of that. While Winter reminds me of a mother, Spring reminds me of the daughter that she has raised and done most of the work for, so she wouldn't have it so hard in life.

After the first ten days, exercise will be a little easier. Your body would have gotten used to feeling sore, and mentally you may have made some awesome breakthrough. This is easy for you now, and during your Summer, you can celebrate. So let's get there!

Sweating it Out in Your Summer

The season of summer is always hot. The days are longer, and sleep seems hard to come by. Maybe it's because of the thunderstorms, or maybe it's because it's too hot to get comfortable. Even though summer is scorching, you can't help but thank God for the beautiful rays of the sun shining down on us. All the flowers are in full bloom and ready to be picked.

Your body's going to have its own little summer. Some of you will be making adjustments in your training, either slowing down or increasing the tempo. That's only because there's a possibility of hitting a plateau. Don't sweat it! Just roll up your sleeve. Summer is hot, but it's one step away from the soothing breezes of your Fall.

Falling in Love with Your Fall

Fall is like no other. She does for all of her girlfriends regardless of their too cold modes, flighty personalities, or volatile eruptions. She lives with the idea of unity in her heart. To go even further, you can call the spirit of Fall, "Love." Her days and nights are equal. She devotes more time to night because she understands that growth takes place when you sleep. While winter sleeps, falls prefers to rest. Fall is Spring and Summer all grown up and touched by Spirit. Physically, she's beautiful; because she's spent time maturing in spirit, and everything that she no longer needs falls away.

As the temperature drops and the summer sun shows less, and as the animals prepare for the seasonal change, a woman in her fall realizes that she is embodying the consciousness to expand herself. All of her trees change colors, and there is a coolness in the air. She began to eat for the maintenance and growth of herself. She makes sure the place for growth is fertile. *It won't be long now*, she says, *until I give birth.*

Ladies, any idea that you wish to make evident on the outer is the idea of giving birth. A lot of you are mothers. Some of you are like me and do not have children. But we do have thoughts; and as women, we have more than enough power to nurture and make them manifest. The seed was planted long ago.

In the process of expressing the body you desire, there will be many seasons. Some will make you question the process. Questioning is good as long as the answers come from you and they feel right within you. God is always helping. So trust yourself and trust the process. *Think right* about this process and *feel good* about each day no matter how volatile it may appear. Go back to Winter and realize that there is something else going on. Go back to Spring and feel happy after your first visual accomplishment, roll with Summer when you start to work to get out of your comfort zone, all the while *understanding* the cycle will lead you to Fall, where you will give birth to your most desired outcome.

Prayer for Departure

Lord God, we just want to thank you in advance for the completion of a successful journey. We see ourselves now as you see us to be, perfect and complete. As we embark upon this journey, we ask that we are renewed both inside and out. Thank you, Lord for our renewal. Thank you for washing away all the thoughts of lack and limitation. We know that the only things that have power over us are the things that we give our thoughts over to. So right now, Lord God, we give our thoughts to Life, Love, Strength, Vitality, Stamina, Endurance, Beauty, Prosperity, and Discipline. We thank you, Lord God, for this time to connect with you. We honor and praise your name as we envision our bodies healthy, radiant, and functioning optimally because they were touched by you. Thank you for being here with us, God, and so it is.

WINTER

WINTER

The universal law for your Winter will be The Law of Success. It is important to understand these laws, so that we can use them for good in our lives. The laws are universal. This means they are working in our lives whether we are conscious that they operate or not. I don't know about you but I'd rather have a say about what plays out in my life rather than live a haphazard existence.

The Law of Success

In his book, 'Working With the Law', Raymond Holliwell describes success as, "a matter of advancement by grade." He says "that no man can become a success except by training." *I like that line.* "An athlete will train for weeks and months to fit himself for a contest that may last for only a few minutes." *I've been there. It's true.* He goes on to say, "The real secret consists in moving forward, and the peculiar mental attitude which promotes this constant progress, is the ruling factor of success."

Whenever I prepared for a show, I became someone else. People around me always assumed something was wrong with me. Now I understand why. It was that peculiar mental attitude. I had latched on to something that only I could see and feel. No matter how much anyone tried to see what I saw, they could not.

What I saw was my family, co-workers, and clients in the audience screaming my name. I saw them running backstage when I was awarded my trophy and crown. I saw myself on the cover of every major health magazine. Then, I was being flown to Chicago to be interviewed by Oprah Winfrey for becoming the first African American Woman to win the figure title at the Olympia weekend. It's like a "Best Body" contest but on an Olympic level. I trained seven days per week and every day I trained, I held that image. It hadn't happened yet; but it was my vision and my desire.

Whenever I was prepping for a show, I tended to my body from head to toe, preserving and nourishing it, for the day of the show. My attitude was that I was already a winner. I was just attending the show to show off, and take home my goodies.

Instead of looking in the mirror everyday and seeing the body I currently had at the time, I painted an image of the body I wanted to express on show day. I saw the one that the judges would say was the winning look, and I focused on that.

During prep time, people like to see the body transform. When people asked me if they could see my body before the final week of the show, I always said no. My reason for not showing spectators my physique was because I did not want a *critique* before the show. No one would throw mud on the image I was creating for myself.

Those who I *trusted*, and were worthy to be on my team, were the ones I went to when I needed to seek advice. At the time, it was my two younger sisters, Aaliyah and Zakiyyah, my coach Frank, my brother Jihad, and my parents, Vicki and Fatih Shakir. For I knew they would be, honest, but they would still encourage me. Some could not understand this attitude; but that was my attitude because *I AM a Winner!* Winners don't pop the champagne until the after party for their victory, and even then, winners who want to remain winners don't get drunk on their success. That was my first National Level Figure Show. I won first place, and qualified to compete on a national level. This is what Holliwell says about it:

"No person can succeed who is not imbued with the desire to advance. In fact, the first step is to become thoroughly saturated with the "spirit of progress" so one feels *stimulated* with a persistent desire to *work* for better and greater things. The desire to advance implies the power to advance. That is the Law as absolute in its actions as any law of science. The fact that you *desire* to succeed is evidence that you have the *power* to succeed; otherwise you would not have been urged to aspire to greatness. You cannot aspire to succeed unless you have the power to succeed. Desire creates the power; power inspires the mind of the individual, and success is the result of that inspiration *rightly* applied."

Wow! Can you believe that all you have to do is *want* something in order for it to show up? I'm going to tell you something better than that. The thing you desire is all already here. It's just waiting for you to *get ready* for it. Some of you don't believe it; but I'm telling you today that it is true! The reason why you can't see your success, in this case we will call it your perfect body, is because up until this point you simply were not ready.

On my way to the library today, I was listening to a tape of one of the church services. I have a bunch of them in my glove compartment in my car just in case I get hungry and need a snack. I grabbed one and slipped it in the tape deck. The lesson was about following your intuition.

I learned that when you follow your intuition, it takes you to your star. That star is your inner knowing. The light that shines in your soul directing you to your highest good at all times. The preacher gave a great definition for the word *ready*. The two words she used were capability and willingness. When the two meet, a person is ready. Only then can they reach their highest good.

It hit home for me, because desire and power are both needed for us to be successful. I'm here to tell you that you would not have the desire to exercise and live a healthier life if the God within you had not given that desire to you. Ideas come from God and living healthy is a great idea! Your desire leads you to this book. That part is done. The question is, are you ready? I know that you are! God knows that you are! But what do you know and believe for yourself? Are you willing to put in the effort? Are you willing to sweat out your perm? Are you willing to turn off the TV for an hour and use that time to exercise? The power within you is and has always been there. You just need to tap into it to make your demonstration. I always say capability is never to be questioned. The very fact that we are related to God makes us more than a conquerer. The question is what lies have you been told and are still telling yourselves, that cripples you and retards your willingness to succeed.

Forget about all the times you bought a gym membership and did not go. Forget about all the money you wasted on Jenny Craig and L.A weight loss. Don't kick yourself because you ran up your credit on an at home gym that you sold in a yard sale for less than ten percent of its purchase price. You were not ready then; *but you're ready now! I can feel it* and I know you can too. *You have the desire again!* So, do the right thing and move forward with it! Don't drop it. If you drop desire too many times she loses her passion and eventually her power is diminished.

The Denial for Winter

The denial for the season is ***There is no evil***. I know that's a big vitamin to swallow. So don't choke. Slowly say it to yourself, and let me explain myself. I know you believe that there is evil because we have the red creature called the devil who rules the hells underneath our feet where all the evil people go right? I'm sorry to throw a wrench in your belief system; that's just not the case. Ask yourself how can there be evil if God is all there is? How can we have evil if God is omnipresence? You've been saying that since you were five years old coming up in the church and now you finally have to account for saying it. Don't sweat it. Here's some ammunition to defend yourself in case your back is ever up against a wall.

You can deny evil on all levels, and do it with confidence. Here's why. God is omnipresence. That means He is everywhere evenly present at all times and in every situation. *Evil* is just the good that we can't see with the two eyes on our face. That good that we can't see, which we refer to as *evil,* is really good waiting for you to recognize it for what it is.

If this is your first time hearing this, it probably sounds like a lot of hoopla; but let me see if I can give you an example. At one of my shows after winning first place, I had to go back out for the overall title. Right when it was time for me to go out for the pose down, my shoes turned up missing. I looked high and low for my shoes but I couldn't find them anywhere. My dad even helped. My sisters were backstage, ready to pull off folks' hair pieces. Meanwhile, my mom was at home praying that my shoes turned up, and I didn't convert back to my old ways. My brother said he didn't like competitions because they bring about things like *this* so he never came.

Anyway, in all the commotion, I found a quiet spot in my head and took three deep breaths. After my dad and sisters were sweating from moving things around looking for my shoes and didn't find them, I accepted the notion that someone had borrowed them without asking and forgot to give them back.

Another competitor offered me hers to complete the show. She was a size nine. I wear a size ten. Imagine me trying to do quarter turns in her size 9 platform 6 inch stilettos. That night I took home one trophy with a big old smile of my face and a sense of accomplishment in my mind. But what plagued me weeks after the show was how someone could be so evil. How could someone do something *like that to me?* I knew I didn't steal anything from anyone. I even brought all of the contestants some chocolate, red wine, rice cakes and peanut butter. So what happened? Why did an *evil* thing like that happen to sweet old Nadirah?

Today, after denying all evil with you all, I begin to see Good/God in that. If that '*evil*' act wouldn't have happened to me, I would still be caught up in trying to win glory through the physical, enslaved to the lowest part of me which is the ego, completely denying my *hearts* true desire which is to write, empower women, and teach truth. Back then, what appeared to be evil really turned out to be good disguised as someone stealing my shoes. That was because those were not the green pastures that God promised me I'd walk in.

GOD IS EVERYWHERE, my friend, even in the worst situations. I'll tell you something else. If I had listened to Him a long time ago when He first spoke to me about my true purpose for this life, I would have never have had to have that experience to begin with. We miss the mark. Our good is always there waiting for us. *There is no evil in the presence of God, and God is present everywhere!* Some of you are still going to try and be logical. My advice is, don't break a sweat trying to figure it out. Save the sweat for your workout. Do *yourself* a favor and except it as truth. What's the worst that can happen; *you begin to see God in everything and in everybody?*

The Affirmation for Winter

The affirmation we'll be working with this season is *God is life, love, intelligence, substance, omnipotence, omniscience, and omnipresence.* Now before you all get to singing your Amen's and things, let's be sure you understand what this means. Let's take the first four words: Life, Love, Intelligence, and Substance. These are all ideas. If you think about each of them for a minute or two, you already have an image of each one.

When I think of life, I think of vitality, strength and energy. I see love as a gentle but powerful force that harmonizes the atmosphere. Intelligence is pure wisdom and inner knowing that you feel in the pit of your stomach. I see substance all around me. Anything that is perfectly formed in the material world is substance. Your body is substance. If you have strength and energy, you represent life. Has the words from your tongue, or your loving smile ever harmonized a chaotic situation? If so, then you are love. God is all of these things, and because we are His children, we have the power to express them.

This is why we can say that God is omnipresence, which means He is everywhere. We are God's children and we are all over the world. Some of us are even in outer space. Even if we are not physically in a place, the work of our Father cannot be put in a box, or confined to a country.

God knows and sees everything. He is omniscience. That's why even when you do something alone with no one else around, you still feel like someone knows. That's why your consciousness starts to bother you. That's only God saying, yes I know about it. Now what do you want to do about it?

The power that we feel, but cannot touch or explain, is the power of God that is all around and within us. This is the omnipotence. This power that we think that we are too little to tap into is already in the palm of our hands, given to us by the master, so that we can make our demonstration.

Now that you have the fundamentals that you'll need for Winter, I have something else for you to do. Yes, there is more work. Getting in shape is about more than an iPod, a stationary bike, and a cute little outfit! It's time to sweat. Before we have our first workout together, I want you to use the jumpstart routine below and complete these exercises. With this session, you can get your mind and body in gear while learning my training style. Another thing about schedules: I prefer to meet with all trainees in the morning for at least the Warm Up and actual exercise. The Cool Down and stretch can be done at night on your own. However, if there are special circumstances, which they always are, don't sweat it. If you need to split up the routine, go ahead. If you have to do it all in the morning or at night, do what's convenient for you. I'm really not concerned with the logistics. I just want to make sure you're getting results. If you are really serious about working out, get up and meet me at the gym at 5:00 am.

The Jumpstart

Warm Up: Remember Success. Go over what it means in your mind until you feel your body start to Warm Up. When you start to feel a little warm, say aloud, There is no Evil. As you get warmer, affirm God is LIFE, LOVE, INTELLIGENCE, and SUBSTANCE. Affirm that He is OMNIPOTENCE, OMNISCIENCE, and OMNIPRESENCE. Your body and mind should be all warmed up now so we can begin.

Exercise: Write down what you want your successful outcome to look like. From head to toe, make notes of the things you wish to change and the things you wouldn't mind staying the same. Put some definition in your abs, if you want. Paint yourself a fresh new coat of acne free skin. Whatever it is you want your body to express, become one with it now.

Cool Down: Read your picture of success aloud first, and then read it to yourself silently. When you feel your heart rate going down, just sit still while inhaling in through your nose and out through your mouth. Meditate on that picture.

Stretch: Expand your consciousness, by contemplating on the word *asceticism*. You will need it for your workout tomorrow. See you then!

Day One: Asceticism

Excellent Morning! How are you? I hope you ate something light. I always try to start my day with 16 ounces of water and some fiber like a piece of fruit. Then, after my workout, I'll have a balanced meal unless I'm cleansing or fasting.

If you feel a little sore from yesterday, don't worry. Today, we're going to exercise another muscle. I try not to work the same muscle back to back, unless it really needs some toning. I call that specialty training. Specialty training is incorporated into my exercise regimen when I've really let things get out of hand, or if I'm preparing for a show. At anytime on this journey if you feel like you want to incorporate specialty training into your exercise regimen, by all means go ahead. You know what you need to work on, so do whatever you feel you need to do, to tighten things up. Always be gentle, though, and careful not to add too much weight before you ready!

As for today our load will be lighter, since we don't have to '*work*' *success, deny* evil, *and affirm what God is*. You all can work with that for the rest of the season if you'd like. Today, we only have to focus on **asceticism**. I promise not to work you to hard. Let's Warm Up!

Warm Up: Concentrate on the word ***asceticism.*** What is your interpretation of it? Once you have conjured up your personal definition, play it back to yourself until you begin to feel warm. While you're warming up, let me give you a basic definition to work with.

Asceticism can be defined as the act of disciplining oneself in an extreme manner. Before you become uneasy focusing on the word *extreme*, understand that extremities are a matter of perception. If I fast on fruit and vegetable juice for this entire journey and ask you to do the same, that may be extreme for most of you. For me, it would not be as hard; because it's an avenue that I've explored before. If I live in Florida, and I visit Chicago on one of their sunny days, a native will surely laugh at me when I walk outside, with my oversized coat, mittens, and head cap. For someone living in one of the hottest states in the world, Chicago's sunny days are extremely cold for me. So let's forfeit our attachment of the word extreme and focus on discipline.

Every religious disciple, every biblical scholar, every historical genius, entertainer or artist, and every great athlete had to come to a point in their lives when they had to strip down to the bare essentials and discipline themselves to make their demonstration. No one can have success without practicing discipline. Focusing your attention, training your mental, spiritual, and physical faculties on the desire that you wish to manifest requires discipline. Most times, it is uncomfortable. This is why it is said to be extreme.

Is it not uncomfortable to tell your friends and family that you cannot accompany them on the family vacation? Is it not uncomfortable to invest the money you saved for the spa getaway on your new endeavor? Doesn't it seem extreme to spend months training and dieting for a show. So it may seem, but in order to accomplish anything worthwhile, asceticism needs to be put into practice periodically to bring forth the manifestation.

Exercise: Make a list of things you can become ascetic in. Abstain from making a long list. Limit it to no more than five things. If there is something on your list that will require more discipline, and more abstaining, focus on that one. Leave room underneath for writing. Use the space underneath to explore reasons why you may be having a difficult time being discipline in that area of your life. Ask for a solution to overcome it when it arises.

Here's an example: I need to practice restraint in my selection of music. The reason I may still like certain types of music is because I may still be harboring the belief that I need to hustle and fight my way through life. A solution to help me overcome this is to affirm that God is Spirit and so am I. Spirit doesn't hustle or fight so neither should I. Then, maybe I can buy an iPod, and program uplifting music.

Cool Down: Review the list and began to prepare for action. Affirm: I AM the ascetic person who continually wills well in my world, life, and affairs.

Stretch: Expand your consciousness by meditating on the word **environment.** Make sure you stretch well. Stretching is something that most athletes forget. Unfortunately, they end up pulling something as a result.

Day Two: Environment

Hey! Hey! Hey! How you feeling? Here's something to think about! Your environment has a lot to do with the way you feel!

Warm Up: Find a quiet place to sit. Take in three deep breaths. In through your nose and out through your mouth. For about ten minutes, close your eyes and reflect on the environment that you would like to see. You can use this time to focus on your home, work place, neighborhood, or country. After you have become one with that picture, open your eyes and affirm, it is so. But hold up! I can't let you off that easy! You got some work to do!

Exercise: Whether the environment you imaged was at home, work, or in your neighborhood or world, you play a tremendous role. Sociology teaches us that every environment starts with the individual.

I told you before that *your* thoughts play a key role in shaping the things around you. This concept is not limited to shaping your gut and your butt. That is mediocre when you think about what your thoughts can do to your environment. Your thoughts affect all of those things that you just imagined. Your home, work, neighborhood, and the world at large are all affected by the thoughts that you put out.

However you imagined your environment to look, it is now up to you to initiate the process, first through disciplined thought, which you started during your Warm Up, and then through action. When you're doing it, cleaning up your environment, shaping it the way you would want it to be, make sure you don't have an attitude that needs readjusting. Adjust it before you begin. In order for anything to happen, you must think "right" about it. You must do the right things to bring it into perfect form, and you must feel good doing it.

If you imagined having more unity in the office you work in, make sure you're not gossiping. If you're not gossiping, be sure you're not listening to gossip. If you are in a conversation and people are gossiping, either excuse yourself or change the topic. If your neighborhood is violent, make sure that you are not contributing by listening to violent music. Make sure you are not beating and cursing at your children. It's all relevant, trust me. If your neighborhood is junky, make sure you keep your house and lawn tidy. It gets contagious. I watched it happen in my own neighborhood. Creating the atmosphere you want, and building the environment you imagine, all starts with you. People are copy-cats. Give them something good to copy.

Cool Down: As an extension of your exercise for today, hold your picture of the environment you'd like to see in mind for another ten minutes. Take a deep breath and affirm that it is so.

Stretch: Expand your consciousness by meditating on the word ***attitude.*** I can see some of yawl rolling your eyes right now. You need to check that, because you'll learn that you can handle anything in life with the right attitude.

Day Three: Attitude

God Bless! Let's Warm Up so we can get right to it.

***Warm Up*:**   Attitude! Attitude…and more Attitude. It's that distinctive gift that every woman has. How can you improve your own attitude? How has your attitude about your fitness goals changed since you've embarked upon this journey? What kind of energy is attached to your attitude as you send it off in the world? Is it positive and optimistic in tone or is it foul and discouraging? Think about these questions while you Warm Up. Also think about the way your attitude has affected the way your body looks and feels thus far.

***Exercise*:**   Answer the questions above in detail before I give you the definition we'll be working with. If you feel you are biased, ask two people who've known you for at least six months to describe the way they perceive your attitude to be. I say two people, because one should be a person you have a lot in common with and get along with fairly well, and the other should be a person who you often agree to disagree with and only speak to if you absolutely must. Trust me, it's good for you!

Here's what happened when I asked a friend to describe my attitude. She told me I had a rebellious attitude. At first, I didn't like the ring to it. Then, I thought about it. It was up to me to keep it or trash it. I chose to keep it. I just changed the negative connotation of the word.

The Oxford Dictionary describes a rebel as "a person who rebels, a person who rises in opposition or armed resistance to an established government or ruler." Now if I would have gotten an attitude with my friend, I would never have discovered what a genius I AM.

After all, she was just telling me what she saw, and she was absolutely right. I was now happy to be this rebel. The way things were going around me, I knew I became this "rebel" to protect myself. My armed resistance really was no firearm at all. Instead, it was the word of truth which I carried in my mind and heart to shield me from those that were in authority and those that still believed in lies and wanted to force them upon me. Learning and understanding universal laws, I had come to realize that I was governed by God. This was easy for me to except because God only wants me to be free and happy.

So don't be upset if someone describes you or your attitude in a negative way. It's your *perception* of it that makes the difference. This brings me to our definition. Your attitude is expressed by your predominant thoughts and feelings. You become settled in that state and you don't even realize it. Now, it becomes mental. When something becomes mental, it will become embedded in you. You have to decide if you want your present attitude to serve you for good or for ill.

Cool Down: Reflect on this. The Revealing Word describes attitude as "*a state of mind, in relation to some matter or situation; a mental position. Attitude of mind toward environment determines the true nature of man's environment. A positive attitude draws the good; a negative attitude brings its train of sin, sickness, poverty, and death. "For as he thinketh within himself, so is he"* (Prov.23:7) It's all about the attitude. What you think in your mind and hold in your heart always comes out whether you like it or not. That appearance is attitude.

Stretch: Expand your consciousness by meditating on the word ***belief***. See you tomorrow.

Day Four: Belief

Top of the morning to you! Are you ready to uncover some things? The best way to do that is to find out what you believe in.

Warm Up: Consider this. The ideas that you have accepted to be true for yourself and others are your beliefs. There are things that you believe that you are not even aware of. Guess what? A lot of the beliefs that you have are not even yours.

Remember we talked about the computer that caught the virus, while being overloaded with everyone else's stuff? The beliefs that you hold on to, that no longer serve to bring you to your highest good, can make you ill as well. This is why it is crucial to clean out that which is not yours first. After you've gotten rid of other people's stuff, it's easier to sort out your own stuff. You can keep what can still be used, and throw out what's no good. Sometimes I keep what others give me if I can use it. My baby sister gave me two beautiful dresses. They look good on me, and they're comfortable too. They were hers, but they serve me, so they're mine now!

Exercise: This is an exercise that you'll probably want to come back to for toning. Find a quiet place where you are. Sit down, and take three deep breaths, in through your nose and out through your mouth. Gently close your eyes. Ask yourself, *what do I believe about myself?* Wait for the answer. Breathe deeply. When it comes, write it down and close your eyes again. Ask yourself, *where did that belief come from?* Wait for the answer. Breathe deeply. Write *it* down. Decide whether that is a belief that came from you or from someone else. If it did not come from you, who did it come from? Does the belief still serve in the advancement of your good? If not, it's time to eliminate it, using denials.

I was born in a Muslim household. My family followed the Sunni teachings. They also accepted a lot of their culture. This included the Islamic dress code for women, and the practice of dating with a witness for the purpose of marriage. At fifteen years old, I was not ready for marriage, but I was ready to experiment with sex.

Going to public school, my parents asked that I followed a moderate Muslim dress code. This meant everything except the head scarf. But when I went to school, I often changed into what was more socially excepted by my peers. Most of my girlfriends had already had sex, and I wanted to know what it was like, especially since I was dating a senior star football player, behind my parents' backs, of course. He had a full scholarship to Florida State University. He would be leaving soon. So he and I made plans to have sex two days before he graduated.

That day finally came and he had sex with me. As I lay on my back, I watched him change one condom after another when my eyes weren't squeezed shut. When he was done, he treated us to lunch at Burger King®. I made it back to school just in time to catch about 30 minutes of my fourth period pre-algebra class. I didn't really understand what just happened, but I felt more grown up.

On my way home on the school bus, all I could think about was burning in hell for all of eternity. Worse than that, what if my parents found out? Not only would I burn in hell for eternity, but my *hide* would be burning *currently*. The only person I told about what I had done was my younger sister, Aaliyah. For about a year, it was our little secret. Although it hadn't happened like I had seen on TV, I wasn't mad about the experience. In fact, thinking about it today still makes me grin.

The more my father read the Holy Scriptures to us after *Sal at*, the more showers I began to take. My vagina was the target. No matter how many baths I took, I was still dirty. *It* was still dirty.

About a year and a half later, my parents read my diary after I had run away to my grandma's house. It was then that they discovered I was no longer a virgin. When I came back, I saw my father cry for the first time. He cried like a child sitting on the floor after *Sal at*. When I spoke to him, he turned his back and went into his room and closed the door. We didn't speak for days. We probably would still not be speaking had I not gone into his room and begged for him to talk to me. I apologized to him, the way mommy suggested I should. For what, I didn't know; but it worked. Looking up from his Koran with tears still in his eyes, he asked me how it felt.

"Like nothing," I said.

"That's because he did not love you, he just wanted to get a feel."

I hugged my father and he did hug me back.

Months later, mommy took me to the doctor for my first pap smear because I felt an itch. The doctor said I had a yeast infection. I'm not sure if it was Candida or toxins from giving birth to a broken heart.

I was raised to believe that sex before marriage was a sin. In the Muslim faith, women who have sex before marriage are dirty and unclean. They are not worthy of receiving a good husband. These women are lucky to have a man be interested in even marrying them.

Needless to say, I felt doomed no matter what I did. So, I acted accordingly. The belief that I was dirty and was to burn in hell stuck with me. Only, I still needed to be held. I still needed to be comforted, and because my father had declined his love for me in so many ways, I ran from one bad relationship to the next. Every time I had sex, I never thought about my own pleasure. As long as he would hold me after he was done, that was enough for me. After every encounter, I thought I was going to get a yeast infection, and most of the time, the *symptoms* were there. In my search for relief, I met a wonderful woman who was a gynecologist, but also someone who studied truth. She was patient, and didn't take my word when I came in with my own self-diagnosis.

"There's nothing there," she said as she moved the light away from the center of me.

"Are you sure? I feel something. It feels itchy and it sort of burns".

"You don't feel anything; it's all in your mind."

"Well, could you still write me a prescription?"

"No, I cannot. If you have no symptoms of a yeast infection, or any other kind of infection, then what would the prescription be for? I was perplexed. "You're fine, so don't worry. Have you ever heard of a book called, You Can Heal Your Life?"

"No."

"When you get a chance, pick it up. The author's name is Louise Hay."

The woman didn't charge me for the visit. Right after I left, I went to pick up the book from Barnes and Nobles. I never had a yeast infection again.

Cool Down: Deny with me: I will not accept any beliefs that no longer serve me. I will not accept any beliefs that cause me to feel lousy about myself. I will not accept any beliefs that do not contribute to my health. I release all that no longer uplifts me.

Stretch: Expand your consciousness by meditating on what it means to **bless**.

Day Five: Bless

Good Morning. Yesterday's exercise was wonderful. Even I felt that. So today will be a bit easier. Nonetheless, it'll still be effective.

Warm Up: Did you think the word **BLESS** was the polite thing we do after someone sneezes. Technically, it can be but you don't have to stop there. Go to a mirror. Look yourself straight in the eyes. Focus on your pupils. Silently, slowly count to ten. When you get to ten, blink once. Refocus your attention on you pupils again, and say "(whatever your name is)", I BLESS YOU. Stay there. Stay focused and then smile. Watch your lips stretch into that beautiful smile. Now you're ready.

Exercise: Let us pray: Lord God, whatever I thought to be wrong in my life today, I am undisturbed by it. I now focus my attention on the blessings that you have bestowed on me. I am now focusing my attention on the blessing I have today. I AM blessed Lord God, and it is all because of you. I AM blessed with Life. I AM blessed with Wisdom. I AM blessed with Intelligence. I am blessed with Prosperity. I AM blessed with Health, and I AM blessed with so much love. I love me. I bless me, and I know you do to, and so it is.

Cool Down: If there is some area in your life that needs to be blessed, invoke your blessing on it now, and release it to God so that spirit can intercede. What you seem to be incapable of, God's blessing can move mountains.

Stretch: Expand your consciousness while you meditate on the word ***chemicalization***. I'll explain it to you tomorrow.

Day Six: Chemicalization

Good morning. Before we begin, I just want to say that I know you all will have a blessed day.

Warm Up: I'm about to take you back. For those of you who have children, you won't have to go back as far.

Remember watching cartoons on Saturday morning as a kid? Remember that crazy scientist who would spend all day and all night in his lab mixing chemical potions. He had tubes on every shelf. There was always that one down on the lab table that he focused on with intensity. It was the one that he claimed would give him the power to rule the world. He would pour an unknown substance into the tube. Slowly, it began to boil and rise. Fizzling to the top of the tube, smoke and steam filled the air. The tables began to shake, and in a scurry, the mad scientist hid under the table. All of sudden, there was a loud BOOM! There was glass everywhere and liquid potions dripping and running down the walls and every table in the lab. The mad scientist slowly crawled from underneath the table. Smiling and fixing his lab coat, he reached for the tube on top of the table which had not been broken. With only a small amount of potion left in the tube, his laugh was filled with a roar. *"For I now have the potion that will help me rule the world."* As if it was his first and last supper, he guzzled the potion. Immediately, he turned into a big, handsome, powerful man. Then he went on to do his work with even more fever, mixing and blending potions that would help others become just as powerful as he had become.

The story of the mad scientist may sound a little bizarre, but in actuality, the same chemical explosion takes place in our minds once we began to think differently. Understanding and learning the truth about who we are can shake things up in our minds if we're not used to this way of thinking. Like the outdated tubes on the shelves that were full of non active potions, negative beliefs and lies are on the shelves in your own mind. The minute someone tells you that you are a child of God, and you are made in His image and in His likeness, and because you are like Him, you are not just a human being, you are a spiritual being, those chemicals in your mind will start to boil. Your outer world will begin to look hazy and foggy, because you will begin to attract situations and people into your world that challenge you. Only then will you put this knowledge to use like the scientist pouring richer, more potent substances of truth into your mind. This will aid in your spiritual growth and development. You will then become resistant to negativity, and what others call chaos. Unfortunately, others will reach for the outdated watered down particles on the dusty shelves, which will not only deplete muscle, but zap both energy and strength. Using those outdated chemicals will stunt and retard any spiritual growth. Here's an example of what chemicalization can look like.

While preparing for my last show, it appeared that my whole world was in turmoil. I couldn't understand why I was filling so miserable inside but looking so tight outside. It was seven days until competition. Looking at my body, I actually believed that I could have competed two weeks ago and had a successful outcome. On my way to the gym that morning, I just couldn't get motivated, so I cranked up Young Jeezy. When he couldn't get me motivated, I cranked up Rick Ross. When he couldn't motivate me, I popped two more fat burners. All of that seemed to pull me further down in the dirt. So I popped in a tape of one of my church services. Why did I do that? The preacher spoke about integrity, something I did not feel I had exercised for the preparation of this show at all. It wasn't just the fact that I had taken the same fat burners I advised my baby sister against. It wasn't even that I was going to allow a panel of judges to validate my beauty again after I had promised myself that I'd never do it again. This time, it had more to do with my purpose. Why was I doing the show?

After trying to coax myself into believing I was doing it to motivate women. The truth is I didn't give a damn who I motivated. I just wanted my trophy and my title. It was true that women would be attracted to a nice physique and it would motivate them to *work out,* but I knew the truth. The truth is ninety percent of the people who get in shape just for looks fall out of shape in less than three months. I also knew that once they fall out of shape, they become depressed, and develop unhealthy eating patterns and become addicted to the supplements they were introduced to that aided them in reaching a desired weight. With me knowing the truth, and on top of that, not having a purpose to do the show, why would I continue? I pulled out of the event and began to really explore what I wanted to contribute to the women as it relates to fitness. Like a scientist, I'm still mixing potions to rule my world, but in the meantime, I refuse to use that watered down stuff.

Exercise: Repeat this to yourself once aloud, and twice in silence. What looks bad is really my good that is not evident to the eyes of man. What appears to be messy chaos is really the universe cleaning and rearranging furniture to make my house in this life a little cleaner and more comfortable. What appears to be a catastrophic eruption was just Mother Nature giving birth to another perfect idea that Father God planted inside of her.

Cool Down: Pray with me. God, thank you for change, no matter how uncomfortable it may be. Even if things look unfamiliar, I know that you are there with me. Amen.

Stretch: Expand your consciousness by reflecting on the word **obedience.**

Day Seven: Obedience

Only an intelligent rebel can appreciate obedience. The conformity it requires turns ugly chaos into beautiful harmony. Obedience is simply submission to law and order. The law is rules and regulations put together by our Lord God to make our life easier. Scripture says that God had given Adam and Eve everything they could desire. He only asked that they not eat of one tree. They were disobedient, and as a result… well you know how the story goes. They are really no rules at all; just universal principles that have always been here for our usage to give us peace and prosperity. The perfect outworking of them by us makes our lives so much smoother, we can't help but notice the order that come in our lives.

***Warm Up*:**   Imagine this if you will. One morning, you wake up to pitch black darkness. You look at your clock and it says 6:30 am. You figure the time must be wrong because it's still dark. You reset the clock and lay back down. An hour later, you wake up again. The clock says 6:30 am. You peak through the blinds, but still utter darkness.

"*What's going on?*" you ask. Before you can slip into your house shoes, the sun answers you back.

"*I'm sick and tired of being sick and tired, and I ain't shining no more for y'all ungrateful butts. Why should I do what I'm supposed to do when everyone else is doing what they want to do.*" Astonished, you pinch yourself and wipe your eyes. Again, the sun responds.

"*This ain't no doggone dream. I'm serious! When you start obeying God, then I'll start obeying God. Until then, try getting to work on time with me taking a week off. See ya!*"

It's not a pretty sight, is it? Imagine going to the beach for a swim, but the ocean sucked itself up, because it no longer wanted to be wet. Surely we would all be lost.

God speaks to each and every last one of us. We continue to do what we want to do so we can reap the accolades. We want our faces to be in the public. We want our names to be highlighted in gold plaques. While we are serving our ego, we are missing out on our true service to God. I would have been an excellent example years ago. I wanted to be in the magazines, and on stage (there's nothing wrong with these things) but God's plan for me was to teach truth and empower the spirit of women behind the pages. It's so ironic, because I always thought I'd be happier in the limelight but my light shines brighter when I serve the Lord. I smile knowing that I can be obedient to God and still pleasure my little ego. You can't lose serving God, no matter how you slice it.

Coming up, I had a real problem with obedience. I didn't like that ugly word *submission* that was attached to it. I didn't like authority figures, and I believed every law was meant to be broken. In elementary school, I got paddles and I stood in the corner. At home, I got whippings and I went to bed early. I was disobedient until I met my seventh grade English teacher, Ms. Black, who recruited me in her speech and debate class. In her class, I could be as disobedient as I wanted, but only on paper and when delivering a speech.

My mother was often the one that would tell me to be obedient. She referred it mostly to my father and the religion. I watched her be obedient to him for many years. I was repulsed by it. She always seemed to be at peace though. Later in their marriage, my father had started to do some things that were not in accordance with the religion and the God that she served. I had never seen my mother disobey my father until that day. It was then that I had come to realize that my father had very little to do with her choice to be obedient. Instead, she was being obedient to God. He just happened to reap the benefits of marrying a wife who was committed to serving a Lord who required submission to her husband.

Exercise: Reflection: Was there a time in your life that you ignored, or disobeyed that still small voice with in? In the pit of your stomach, you knew that the voice you heard was guiding you to do something the Lord asked of you. Did you obey? Were you disobedient? If you obeyed, remind yourself of God's grace. Look around and take note of the enlargement of your territory. If you haven't reaped the visual rewards of your labor yet, exercise faith. Use this time to affirm the expansion of your good. It is on its way. If you were ignorant then, forgive yourself. Listen to that steady quiet voice within. God may still want you to travel that same road, or there could be a different path all together. It has been my experience that if God has something He wants done by you, it's never too late. He only requires that you get started; and He sends angels from everywhere to help you get the job done. It's never too late to be obedient.

Cool Down: Affirm: I am obedient to God in my world and affairs. (Repeat silently 20 times)

Stretch: Expand your consciousness by reflecting on the word **give**.

Day Eight: Give

Warm Up: Answer this question. Are you a giver or a taker?

When I was younger, I heard someone say fat people are greedy. At the time, I could not grasp the concept. As I got older however, I began to understand why someone would say a thing like that. What that person really meant to say was that people who are overweight have problems letting go. They take in more than they let go; or they take and store what no longer serves them.

The *fat* we see is really *energy* stored up for later use. My only disclaimer is that more than often fat is negative energy stored in excess. Most people understand this. Consciously, they hold on to it, realizing that negative energy stores require the most work to release. Unconsciously, they don't even want to release it. They realize that, in releasing it, things can get ugly. This is because the energy associated with fat is almost always repugnant. In a way, it's like fat people say, I'd rather hang on to it than have someone else be bothered with it. This is exactly the time that you want to turn a negative into a positive. By doing that, it would be easier both physically/subconsciously, and mentally/consciously to release that which no longer serves you for your highest good.

In my experience, I've discovered that people who are overweight are not greedy, they're just afraid to let go. In other words, they are great receivers, but they rarely release anything. They carry around their own hurts, and pains, as well as those of others, whether it is those of friends or family members. This is an unhealthy practice for anyone, and it directly retards the law of receiving. The law of receiving states that you must give just as much as you want returned to you. This giving and receiving process creates a healthy balance keeping positive energy free flowing. In the body, the law of giving and receiving looks like a healthy metabolism, increased energy, stamina, and a healthy digestive system. The key is putting in the right fuel to keep the vehicle running smoothly.

In the body, unhealthy use of the law of giving and receiving looks like both constipation and irritable bowel syndrome. With constipation, you are unable to release. With irritable bowel syndrome, you want to release but you cannot. So you hang on until you explode. It also shows up as obesity, which is storing too much, or bulimia and anorexia, which does not know how to accept and receive graciously that which is nourishing. It is important to use the law of giving and receiving correctly in terms of our bodies. It is also paramount that we conclude to use this law justly in our life, world and affairs; because what you give, you will receive. So, give that which promotes a healthy life in all areas, and you shall be blessed accordingly.

Exercise: Answer these questions. If I am a giver, what am I giving? How do people respond to what I give? When I give, do I expect something in return? Am I dependent on praise, recognition, or even a thank you from the person or cause I give to? Why am I giving? Am I giving for the love of giving or am I giving to get or because I feel obligated?

If you are a receiver, what do you receive? Are you accustomed to receiving something in particular? Do you receive so much that you feel like you can share with others? Are the things that you're receiving building you up in terms of health, radiance, and promotion? Is that which you receive depleting you, or having you feel burdened? Would you give that which you receive to someone you love?

Answer these questions and you should be able to identify if what you are giving and receiving is for your highest good. If it is so, continue in that path. If it is not, it's never too late to change.

Cool Down: Affirm: I only give what uplifts those around me. I only receive that which can promote me to my highest good.

Stretch: Expand your consciousness by reflecting on the word **doubt**.

Day Nine: Doubt

Good Morning, my radiance. Shall we begin?

Warm Up: Close your eyes. Take three deep breaths, in through your nose and blow them out slowly through your mouth. What is your childhood dream? Take a few moments to think about that. Close your eyes and become one with your dream. Can you feel it? Picture your dream the way you want it to come into manifestation. Feel your cheek bones rising because you cannot stop smiling about your dream. Picture yourself enjoying your new life now because of the dream. Feel yourself immersed in the fullness of your dream. You are doing it. You are doing it, and you are doing it so well. Take a deep breath and open your eyes. *Now let's face reality.*

YOU CAN'T DO THAT! WHO TOLD YOU THAT YOU WERE GOOD ENOUGH TO DO THAT? YOU DON'T HAVE ENOUGH MONEY FOR THAT! YOU DON'T HAVE A COLLEGE DEGREE! WHO'S GOING TO HELP YOU! YOU'RE A SINNER! GOD HATES SINNERS! SO GOD HATES YOU! YOU ARE A LOSER! WHY ARE YOU TRYING TO GET IN SHAPE? YOU WERE BORN FAT. YOU'LL ALWAYS BE FAT! GO GET A BOWL OF ICE CREAM WITH EXTRA FUDGE, AND WHILE YOU'RE AT IT, ORDER A PIZZA! YOU CAN'T EVEN LOSE 10 POUNDS!

I assume you're all warmed up, now let's exercise.

Did you know that there are only two emotions? Those two

emotions are fear and love. Love is the energy that attracts, binds, and harmonizes all things. Love promotes health, beauty, wealth, and joy. Fear stagnates, divides, and criticizes. Out of fear come hate, jealousy, depression, and DOUBT.

Doubt is the opposite of assurance which is our inheritance from God. I once had a client of mine who was very persistent in trying to sell me life insurance. At twenty seven, this life insurance sounded more like death insurance. Consciously I wasn't thinking about dying anytime soon. When I told her, I wasn't interested, she wanted to know why.

"I plan on living a prosperous, long, healthy life, and when the time comes that I make my transition, I'll have more than enough money to afford me a proper burial. Besides, my transition ceremony will have a closed casket, so I don't need the makeup and fancy clothes."

She just stared at me as if I were already gone. As she gathered her things, I couldn't help but wonder why someone was so adamant in trying to sell 'death insurance' to a perfectly healthy, and might I add radiant 27 year old truth student. I know some of you are probably saying she was just doing her job; but because I study truth I question what appears to be the most random act. I was a person who valued life and openly declared health and wholeness, so what was I missing? Did I doubt my own belief?

On my way home, I asked God to reveal to me why someone was trying to sell me death insurance. I could come up with nothing except that the lady was just doing her job. That was a watered down answer. I gave myself more time for understanding.

Finally, my answer came to me. For months, I had been contemplating stepping out on faith and taking the time off to pursue what I am doing at this very moment. The discrepancy was that I doubted myself the whole way through. I thought that if I took time off from my job, I'd lose money, status, and eventually die from brokenness. It sounds extreme, but if you think about it why else do we panic, and become frantic about losing our jobs? It is because somewhere deep down in the depth of your soul, you believe you won't be able to buy the things you need to keep you alive, and as a result of that lack, you'll eventually die. The death insurance lady had come to sell me my very own belief. Her trying to get me to buy death insurance was my belief in lack, defeat, need, and eventually death coming to the surface. At the time, I believed I needed the insurance that my job provided.

For the record, I must say that I do love my job. Not many can say that, but I can. I hear people complain about the people they work with and their careers in general. Whenever I hear that, I realized just how blessed I am to work with, and work for something I love and believe in. I'm always joyful when I motivate and empower people in life, so for this, I give God praise. However, in working in such a physical environment, I have noticed that people get so caught up in what they see in the mirror that they neglect their mind and spirit all together. It was put on my heart to help those that wish to achieve physical strength become cognizant of the inner strength as well.

Exercise: Deny with me: There is not a doubt in my mind that I can accomplish anything I put my mind to. God has promised me the kingdom, and that is all the assurance I'll ever need. I move forward with my heart's desire knowing that it is already done. And so it is. (Repeat 5 times aloud in front of a mirror. Be sure to look yourself square in your eyeball)

As an extension, write this affirmation down once using all capital letters. Then underneath it write out your lifelong dream.

Cool Down: Recite your denial three times silently, using the following 3 step guide: Sit quietly with your eyes close. Repeat denial once. Take a very deep breath. Take a couple of minutes to visualize yourself doing what you love. (Repeat process two more times)

Stretch: Expand your consciousness by meditating on the word ***intuition***.

Day Ten: Intuition

I have that feeling. It's that feeling deep down in the pit of my stomach that we are going to get so sweaty; we'll all need new perms. Because I love me some intuition, I exercise it regularly.

***Warm Up*:**   You can do this exercise sitting or standing. If you're sitting down, I prefer that you sit in a chair. Be sure both feet are planted flat on the floor and are shoulder width apart. Be sure that your back is straight. Open both hands and place the right hand just above your navel, and the left just below it. Breathe deeply, and slowly. If you are lying down, be sure you are on your back. Separate your feet slightly, making sure they are shoulder width apart. Open both hands. Place the right hand just above your navel, and the left just below. Apply the same breathing.

                When your body is totally calm, say this, *I am now in touch with my feeling nature. Everything I need to know is at the center of me.*

Intuition is that inner knowing that resides deep down at your core level. It is not attached to past experiences, statistics and opinions. Most of the time, it is not supported by our intellect. Intuition is our God-intelligence. It is our personal navigation system and our road map to our highest place in life. When we follow our intuition, we come into a place of peace, joy and wholeness.

Here's a story about two friends, one named Nadirah and the other Aqueelah. Seven years ago, Nadirah met a handsome, charming, well-to-do fellow. Her entire body sang when the charming fellow approached her. Although she admitted that certain parts of her were singing off-key, she hummed along because her lower body was singing a catchy chorus.

Nadirah introduced her new beau to her friend Aqueelah. Aqueelah wasn't impressed. In fact, she told her that something wasn't quite right. Nadirah accused her trusted friend of being jealous and trying to sabotage her one chance of living the *good* life. Aqueelah was heartbroken. Couldn't her friend see she was just concerned? Didn't Nadirah understand that Aqueelah was just trying to help her stay her course and accomplish the goals she set for herself?

Obviously not. Nadirah had become disgruntled, yelling for her friend to shut up. She called her lifelong friend confused and mentally deranged. She said she was irrational and stupid. Aqueelah was saddened by the way her friend had turned on her. Had she forgotten the times she saved her from Moe, Joe, Tom, Sam, Billy, Henry, Dave, and Josh? Why was she acting this way? Nadirah had tuned her out completely.

Aqueelah suffered a terrible wound to the heart. If she was going to save them, she needed time alone to strengthen herself. Reluctantly, she left Nadirah to her own logic. She went away for a couple of months. Every now and then she would call Nadirah, but Nadirah would never respond to her. How could she when the charming stranger was always whispering sweet nothings in her ears? Aqueelah's voice was almost silenced in her efforts to yell over the voice of the charming stranger, Nadirah's fluttering heart, and pulsating vagina. So, she did what most friends do when their friend just doesn't listen. Aqueelah prayed for her friend.

"God, thank you for blessing Nadirah to recognize that everything that shines is not always diamonds. I know she cannot see that with the eyes on her face, so I ask that you bless her with a discerning heart. Lord, when she is ready, let her call for me. Amen."

It had been almost two years since Nadirah heard from Aqueelah. Whenever she thought she heard Aqueelah, the voice was silenced by a phone call from the charming stranger, a fancy trip out of town, new outfits, shoes, jewelry, and body heat. Every once in a while, though, Nadirah remembered her friend. When the charming stranger was out of town on business, she'd try and find her. Sitting in one of the empty rooms of the charming stranger's house, she closed her eyes and called for Aqueelah, but it was a waste of time. Aqueelah had abandoned her and she had every right, after the way Nadirah had treated her.

One day, while the charming stranger was away on business, Nadirah found her friend Aqueelah in a dream. Seeing the stranger in a foreign place with another woman was enough to bring Nadirah to her knees. Instantly, Aqueelah met her there. It was like yesterday. They hadn't missed a beat.

"Aqueelah, your voice is different, you sound older."

"Well it's been almost three years. So technically, I am more mature. *Not* only that, but your voice does tend to change if you've been yelling."

"I'm sorry if I made you yell; but I need your help. Something's not right with the charming stranger. I need to get out of here."

"I see this is no time for I-told-you-so, but what about the pact we made never to move in with a man unless we were married?"

"Come on, Aqueelah, we're talking about living in a new development, with 5 bedrooms, a two-car garage, three bathrooms, including a his-and-hers bathroom, a huge kitchen, my own private office, and a closet so big I can live in it if I wanted to as opposed to mom's house in a room no bigger than his closet."

"Okay, but are you comfortable here?" Nadirah was silent. Aqueelah continued. "Are you *really* happy about this move? Are you even still in school? Why aren't you working and supporting yourself? That's not like you."

Tears began to roll down Nadirah's face when she realized that this was not *her* life at all. Because she was focusing on survival, she forgot how to live. Now, in her effort to survive, she was dying and she was the one with the murder weapon. All the things that made her happy, she was no longer doing. She remembered her dreams, and the promises she and Aqueelah had made together. When she met the stranger, one by one, the dreams fell away from her like the leaves fall in autumn. Aqueelah was still there. Nadirah could hear her breathing.

"So what do I do now?" she humbly asked Aqueelah.

"You get some rest. I've had enough rest. Let me carry us for a while."

"What about your heart? Is it still broken?"

"Don't you know I'm invincible? I've been doing this before your little body even came into expression. I've been yelled at. I've had plates thrown at me. Once, there was a lady who began pounding her head and shouting for me to come out."

"Did you get out?"

"Of course not, I just shut up for a while, and came back when she was a bit calmer. I didn't want her to hurt herself. My job is to protect you even from yourself. If you get quiet enough to listen, I can give you directions to find my friend *Purpose*. He's really cool. *Joy* and *Peace* hang out with *Purpose* too. *Love* cooks us all dinner, and her husband *Truth* serves it to us."

"Why haven't I met any of those guys?"

"I don't know, maybe it's because you never let me lead."

"So I guess you're leading me out of here, right?"

"Right!"

"Do I have to go back to mama's house?"

"Well, being that you have no money of your own, no job, and no education, it's either mama's house or walking the streets for a couple days while we come up with a plan. One thing that I do know is that we have to get you out of here. So what's it going to be mama's house, or the streets?"

"Let's do mama's house. I'll be looking for a job, first thing tomorrow"

"Great! I'll drive. You can relax. I know the way!"

Aqueelah helped Nadirah pack up all of her things from the charming stranger's house. Nadirah was tempted to trash the place before she left, starting with the plasma TV and its surround-sound, and then moving to the snow white baby grand piano. Aqueelah helped her see that trashing the place would do more harm than good. She reminded Nadirah that she also played a role in her unhappiness. Nadirah agreed. She and Aqueelah drew up a letter for the charming stranger and left it in the big kitchen on top of the microwave, along with the key to the stranger's house, and the 2 ½-karat diamond platinum ring. The letter read.

>Dear Charming Stranger,
>
>I hadn't planned on leaving like this, but then again I hadn't planned on leaving at all. I feel like my life has no purpose, and as a result of that something in me is dying. This is not your fault. You gave me the things that you thought would make me happy. The truth is happiness cannot be made, or found in things. Happiness is a state of mind, one that I have been trying to obtain by manipulating things outside of me. In my efforts to do so, I attracted you into my life. It is what it is. As for the relationship, we both made mistakes, some big some small, but I want you to know that I hold nothing against you. Throughout this relationship, I've observed our individual strength. I've had many good times with you, and we've made memories that I will not forget. Whether our

relationship was built on love, all depends on the observer's definition. As for my own self, I believe I fell in love with the idea of having someone express so much of what looks like love on me. I would ask you to wait for me until I have everything figured out, but time, like intuition, is one of our closest friends and should not be taken for granted. So I will say this. I love you for all that you have been to me. Up until this point, you have been my greatest teacher. There are some lessons in which I am still digesting. I wish you the best in your life. As for myself, I have work to do, so I am moving on. However I'll always be with you in spirit.

Love Nadirah

P.S. Don't forget to smile. You look best when you smile.

Nadirah wanted to leave some sexy pictures of herself with the note, ring, and letter just in case, the charming stranger really thought about leaving "business" to be with her. Aqueelah advised her that if it was meant to be, it will be. With that, she picked up the photos, tore them in tiny pieces and trashed them.

It was not easy for Nadirah to get on her feet. Her bank account was at -$100. People were talking about how stupid she was for waiting so long to leave the charming stranger. She had to settle back in with her mom and sisters which was *always* a work in progress. Before she could enroll in college again, she had to past the same math test she tried to get around before she started dating the charming stranger. She was a couple thousand dollars in debt, because of maxed-out credit cards. She felt lonely, stupid and angry, and she missed the body heat of the charming stranger. She didn't know what to do or where to begin. Moving the boxes and bags out of her way, she found a spot on the cold tile in her room and she prayed.

"Father God, show me what to do from here, whatever You say do I'll do. Just get me up from here. In this I pray, Amen."

This time intuition had led her to Holy Spirit and Father God, and they began to work with her. She had to find a place of worship that was her first thing. Aqueelah was cool with that because that increased her strength. She enrolled in some classes at her church to understand more about the *roll* she played in her experience with the stranger. Both Aqueelah and Nadirah liked the classes because they served them both. Nadirah liked them because she learned that she can *control* things through thought, and Aqueelah liked them because all of her friends seemed to be there. The Universal Truth Center was pleasing to the both of them. Nadirah began to trust Aqueelah again and let her lead their way.

For a year, they focused on studies at Nadirah's university and studies at the spiritual center. They earned money by using her personal training skills as an independent trainer. Three weeks later, Nadirah-Aqueelah landed a new job at a very prosperous fitness establishment about five minutes from her house. It was there that she met the same woman in her dream. The woman claimed she was engaged to the charming stranger, and they had been seeing each other for almost a year. Nadirah cried, but Aqueelah helped her wipe her tears and gave her strength to carry on.

Exercise: Affirm aloud. Repeat three times. I surrender everything that looks like truth, and I now feel the truth. I listen for the small voice inside of me and follow its instruction.

Cool Down: Repeat your Warm Up.

Stretch: Expand your consciousness by focusing on the word **peace**.

SPRING

SPRING

The Law of Thinking

The Law of Thinking will be our focus this season. The average person thinks about any and everything that is introduced to her, whether it is good or bad. We think about what we hear on the news or what happened last year. Have you ever even thought about what it means to think right? I know you're thinking, *how in the heck am I supposed to think right with so much going wrong?* This is what it means to think right. Paint a picture of everything good you want to happen in your life. Try spending ten minutes a day for the remainder of this season just thinking about it. This is a good way to start. I'm not saying that bad things will not happen. What I am saying is that once you learn to think right, it will become easier to focus on the smallest good thing. That small good thing will create a mountain of good.

Here's an example of right thinking. Say your goal is to lose thirty pounds. The first thing you should do is say, "Thank you God for my losing thirty pounds." Then see your body in your desired perfect form. Once you get that picture, a thought may enter your mind, *you can't get that body because you are not 21 anymore.* Simply push that thought aside and picture your desired body again. Hold it in your mind and say aloud to yourself, "Please to yourself, girlfriend, I do not need to be 21 to sport a body like a 21-year-old. I can do it right now."

Think about it. Work towards it, and feel darn good doing it. Stay away from disbelievers, and before you know it, people will be carding you at the door of your favorite dance club.

Denial for the Spring

Let's say it together. "There is no absence of life, substance, or intelligence anywhere." If this is a challenge to believe, remember this.

God is Life, Substance, and intelligence, and God is always around right? Let's take a deeper look at these ideas individually. Life can never be absent even if something seemingly dies. I like to use the word transition, because I don't believe anything really dies because whatever *dies,* something seems to always grow in its place.

Old hair falls out, new hair grows in. A person dies, but has children and as an extension they live on. Even if you are like me and have no children you will still live on in the minds and spirits of those who you've touched and inspired while living. Jesus is an excellent example of that. He had no children yet His spirit lives on in many. Life is never absent because ideas will forever be flowing through all of mankind. If our ideas are good, we will live *"the good life."*

Substance is just our desires and ideas coming into expression in the material world in perfect form. For relation sake, we can refer to things like food, shelter, money, and your new body as substance. These material things are ideas given to man by God to bring them into material manifestation. No matter how fancy we remodel the Mercedes Benz, it's still an idea of transportation, which came from our two legs and feet, then the camel, then the horse and carriage.

Man upgrades substance. The original idea of substance will always be here. If we like our comfort and convenience, it is up to us to love and respect the things that we have now in order to receive more. By that I mean nature itself. We can't expect to tear up God's original idea of housing which is the earth, and throw trash and garbage all over it and expect to live in a beautiful, luxurious home. Once we learn to respect the idea of substance, we can watch more of it materialize in our lives. It may be a work in progress for some, but it is definitely worth a conscious effort because that is where our resourses to build more come from.

YOU AND I ARE INTELLIGENCE. Don't be fooled by your foolish decisions. View intelligence this way. Whether or not we drink water, the human body is composed mostly of this vital substance.

We drink water; we bath, wash our hair, and brush our teeth using water. If we drink more water, there's a great possibility that our bodies will function more efficiently. Just like water, our intelligent factor is within us. It is safe to say that we are made up of intelligence. We can use it and have our lives flow smoother or we can ignore it and let it remain dormant. In either case, it is there waiting for you to use it or add to it. Let's deny together. "There is no absence of life, substance, or intelligence anywhere, because God is Omnipresence. Furthermore there is no absence of life, substance, or intelligence, because I am an intelligent being who is full of good ideas; and I have the power to give life to any idea of substance that I wish to create."

Affirmation for Spring

"I am a child of God, and every moment His life, love, wisdom and power flow into and through mc. I am one with God and I am governed by His Law."

Wisdom is another form of intelligence. Intelligence gives us the power to bring the never ending flow of good into our lives. Once we have that beautiful flow in front of us it is time for us to jump right in the pool of abundance. The pool of abundance is one of the many amenities to the Lord's mansion. We are children of God and He has given us the master key which unlocks every door in the mansion. We can live in His mansion for the rest of our lives or we can stay cramped up in a wretched shack. The key is ours to unlock any room in the mansion we desire, and there will still be room for our brothers and sisters too. Our Father God is a good provider, and we are blessed that He doesn't believe in retirement!

Exercise in Spring will be a bit different than Winter's regimen. In Winter, I accompanied you in our Warm Ups, Exercises, Cool Downs, and Stretches. I wanted to ensure you were safe and understood the process. This season, I won't be meeting you for Warm Ups. You'll

Warm Up alone. Just to recap on Warm Ups, simply spend 15 minutes with yourself in silence. Use this time to study your lessons from Winter. If you followed both mental and physical instructions for Winter exercises, you should be in good condition and ready for a rather progressive Spring.

As I mentioned in the beginning, this is a 40 day program. If you feel the need to spend more time in Winter for any part of the program, do so. You know what your mind and body needs. Take your time! Remember, being patient with yourself is a good sign that you love yourself. For those of you who are ready to move on, there's a sample exercise below. Those of you who are going to spend more time in Winter, I'll see you when you're ready for Spring! God Bless!

Sample Work Out for Spring

Exercise: For the rest of the day, think right! Today, make a conscious effort to think positive thoughts. If something happens in your daily routine that does not look good, search for something positive in that situation.

Cool Down: Repeat your denial and affirmation for this season six times each. Three times aloud, and three times in silence: "There is no absence of life, substance, or intelligence, anywhere." "I am a child or manifestation of God, and every moment His Life, Love, Wisdom, and Power flow into and through me. I am one with God and I am governed by His Law."

Stretch: I did not forget about PEACE.

Day Eleven: Peace

Welcome to Spring!

Warm Up: Center yourself by taking three deep breaths in through your nose and out through your mouth. Affirm five times, "Peace be still in my life."

I was headed to class one morning. As I got off I-95, rain came pouring out of the sky like the falls of Niagara. Lightning began to strike left and right, and thunder was clapping, like folks heard the president had announced the war was over and our soldiers were all coming home. "It's just a storm", I tell those around me who seem to be running for cover. However, today was a little different. I'll be honest. *Today was a whole lot different.*

As I got off the expressway headed to 125th street, the rain poured harder and harder. The lightning was striking as if *I* were its target. I could not even hear the radio from the thunder clapping so loudly. The tapping on the hood of my car made me turn my radio down. Two seconds later, it sounded as if someone were throwing golf balls at my car, deliberately trying to break out my window. I looked up and I could see nothing but gray. I was blinded by the rain. My only two choices were to stop smack dab in the middle of traffic on a slippery road or continue to drive without the comfort of sight. The only thing that I could think of was hitting someone else and causing them pain. Slowly, I came to a halt. Pressing my emergency lights, I waited with my hands balled in a tight fist. My eyes were squeezed shut, and my heart was beating like an African drum on Kwanzaa. It was beating so loud I could hear it over the thunder. My heart was beating so hard, I saw my t-shirt jumping.

Suddenly, in the midst of the confusion, I felt a peace come over me. Spirit had whispered to me "*Relax. this is not your storm.*" When I heard those words, my fist opened up, as did my eyes. As trees obeyed the wind, and swayed in whatever direction she commanded, they showed me mines. A gas station just a couple of lanes away beckoned me to pull into a spot that looked as if the storm had not touched. As I shifted the gear into drive and released my heavy foot from the brake, I felt my car shake as if it was as light as a salt shaker. I began to tense up again. Then the voice came back again. "Relax, this is not your storm. I began to chant. "*Peace be still. Peace be still. Peace be still.*" I recited that until I began to feel my heart rate slow down. As I pulled in the driveway, I became calm again. I realized that nothing, I don't give power to, can harm me. If there is peace in me, I could always find a peaceful place even when things are not so peaceful.

Exercise: Take out your writing utensils. Write the following 10 times. I AM PEACE.

Cool Down: Take three deep breaths and whisper the following 20 times. Peace be still in my mind, life, world and affairs.

Stretch: Expand your consciousness by reflecting on the word **strength**.

Day Twelve: Strength

Strength is not solely limited to the size of your bicep. It is not only measured by the amount of weight you lift in the gym. Strength is our God given energy. Being strong means that you exemplify integrity; despite the fact that it may be easy to follow the crowd. Gaining strength is a process and not everyone arrives at the same time. Spiritual strength is gained in stages just like physical strength. Understand that strength is a combination of physical, mental, and spiritual expression.

I consider us friends now, so I'm going to share some of my personal business with you. I've been celibate for three years now. For me, that takes a heck of a lot of strength. It's a no brainer...*Sex Sells!* Major marketing companies know this and that's why subliminal messages aren't subliminal at all. They ooze sex. Have you ever seen one of those old Coke® commercials where the hot and sweaty cowboy takes off his shirt? The tall, thin brunette licks her ruby red lips as she slips an ice cold Coke® in his rough masculine hands. The tip of the bottle adds moisture to his dry lips. With every gulp, his Adam's apple gyrates as he quenches his manly thirst. The slender brunette watches with anticipation as she bites her bottom lip as to say, "Can I have some?" Giving her the half-empty bottle, she put her mouth where his has already been and begins to suck as if this were her last drink. After their thirst has been quenched, they walk into the sunset, his arm around her neck, her hand in his back pocket. And you wonder why you can't kick the Coca-Cola® habit!

I chose to abstain because I realized I had never been intimate with myself, let alone had connected with myself physically, mentally, *and* spiritually. It takes a great deal of strength to face yourself, and love yourself even if you don't feel loving. It's easy to jump into the arms of someone else to escape your pain. When you're in pain, it's easy to confuse good sex with love. Looking yourself in the eyes and finding love there when you're in pain takes a lot of spiritual muscle.

Exercise: Affirm with me. God is the source of my strength. With Him by my side, I can move mountains.

Cool Down: Pray with me: God, thank you for making me strong enough to do what I came to this world to do. Amen

Stretch: Expand your consciousness with the word ***friend***.

Day Thirteen: Friend

My mother hung a plaque in our utility room when I was about twelve. The plaque read, "*A FRIEND IS SOMEONE WHO STEPS IN WHEN OTHERS STEP OUT.*" What a weak definition for the word friend, I thought. Wasn't it supposed to say something about a friend being in your life forever, and hanging out with you on the weekends, and loaning you money? That's not what it said. I believe I met one of my best friends when I met a man named Frank.

I call Frank my coach because he helped me get ready for a show. He's about 50-something and he has so much wisdom about life. If I have a question about anything, I call Frank. I call him my couch because he doesn't believe in giving answers. He'll give me information and direction so that I can make an informed decision. I'll never forget when he coached me for my show. He always said, "If you're going to make a career of this, I want you to learn the ins and outs." Then he would bring me all of this reading material on nutrition and contest prep. At first, I was annoyed, and I thought why doesn't he just tell me what to do. I finally realized that friends empower each other, not debilitate each other.

Before I met Frank, there was another guy who used to train me. He acted very domineering, not wanting me to talk to anyone but him about diet and exercise. When I went to get my certification to be a trainer, he acted as though I had done something wrong. This was not the friendship I wanted.

My mother's plaque was right. Friends are just like angels that are sent by God to help you along the way. They can be in your life forever or just for one day. You can identify a true friend when they display patience and generosity. They are motivating and encouraging. In a friendship, there is a positive exchange of energy and both parties involved benefit from the union. Later, I learned that Frank was a smoker, and was trying to quit. Him encouraging me to be healthy and strong helped him kick his habit.

Exercise: You will need a paper and pen for this exercise. List three of your closet friends. Answer these questions. How did we meet? What did we have in common then, and does that commonality still stand? Does this commonality empower me to be the very best me I can be? If you answered yes, that's great, if you answered no then you have some letting go to do. A denial may be a good way to start. You can say something like this: I release all things and all people which are not good for my life. How do you feel when you are around your friends? Do you feel drained, bored, competitive, or uneasy? These are not good signs. You may need to repeat the same denial. What do you talk about with your friends, people, events, or ideas? If you find that you're talking about people, you may want to try changing the discussion to events or ideas. The old expression goes something like this, small minds talk about people, average minds talk about events, and great minds discuss ideas. Friends should help you expand your awareness, not limit it.

Cool Down: Pray with me: God, thank you for making me a good friend, and thank you for sending good friends my way. Amen

Stretch: Expand your consciousness by reflecting on the word ***scarcity***.

Day Fourteen: Scarcity

Do you support the idea of scarcity? Here's one way to find out. Ask yourself, have you ever verbalized and thought like this:

1. There's not enough time in a day. Time flies. I don't have enough time.

There are twenty four hours in a day, seven days in a week, and 365 days in a year. That sounds like more than enough time to get anything that needs to get done, done! When Spirit is working with us, we are not bound by standard time. We are on God's time and God's time is abundant.

2. No one supports me. You just can't find good help.

There is always someone that is willing to help and support you in anything you desire to do. It looks as if no one is there to help because we have our minds set on the people we want to help us, or we feel are obligated to help us. God sends angels all the time to help us on our journey. We don't recognize them because we're looking for someone else.

3. There are no more good men. There are no more good black men. They are either gay, on drugs, or locked up.

I work around eligible black men all day. Some of my best friends are black men, and they are not in jail, nor do they have a criminal record. They don't use drugs, and they are not homosexual. Women always say they want a good man. Yet, they sit around with their girlfriends and refer to men as dogs, broke-niggas, trifling, and hoes. I don't understand this. This may be a big vitamin to swallow but I remember when I was running into dogs, I was behaving like an animal. If I did run into a broke *nigga,* I was probably dependent on the wealth of someone else instead of trying to create my own. All I'm saying is that you attract what you are at the time. Now, I meet some of the most handsome, educated, prosperous, God-like men, and it's not because I changed my location, it's because I am changing my state of mind.

4. I don't have enough money. I'm broke. I can't afford that. That's too expensive for my blood.

How could something be too expensive for your blood, if you are a child of God? How can you not have enough money when God has given you the kingdom? You become susceptible to this way of thinking when you fail to explore the gifts and talents that have been given to you by God. Exploring your gifts and talents will keep you in the flow of abundance, because when you explore your gifts and talents you began to realize that *you* are the producer. The view you have of yourself shifts from beggar to creator.

Creators constantly think of ways to bring the desires of their heart into manifestation. It is the creator's repetitive thought process that produces the experience needed for the demonstration of the creator (thinker) to be made. So once you begin to view yourself as a creator instead of a beggar, the Universe will respond by sending you the experiences you need so that you can exercise your natural gifts and talents. When we are using our natural gifts and talents, we awaken our divine potential, and our divine potential is limitless just like God.

Exercise: Grab your pen and pad so that you may answer these questions. Do I have a scarcity mind set? What areas of my life am I experiencing lack and limitation? What can I do to change? Before you rush to answer these questions, be sure to take a thorough inventory. Sometimes, the beliefs of lack and limitation are buried so far down in the subconscious that we don't even recognize that they are playing out in our lives.

After you have identified the areas in your life where you are experiencing lack, use denials and affirmations together to erase thoughts of limitation, and to attract more of what you want in your life. Here's an example: lack of time. I do not lack any time. I use the time that I have wisely. I am infinite. I have all the time in the world.

Cool Down: Pray with me: God, thank you for a prosperity consciousness. Thank you for giving me everything I desire. Thank you for plenty of money, plenty time, and plenty friends. Thank you for awesome health, and the remembrance that you have given me the kingdom. All I must do is walk in. Amen.

Stretch: Expand your consciousness with the word ***gratitude***!

Day Fifteen: Gratitude

Gratitude is simply the act of giving thanks. Giving thanks put you in a positive state of mind because it makes you aware of all the wonderful things you've been blessed with. When you are feeling grateful, you become more receptive to all that is good. Yesterday, we talked about complaining about what you don't have and how it creates more lack in your life. To emphasize that, I say this, you cannot be truly grateful if you are struggling with scarcity. It's a contradiction. Either you're thankful and faithful or you're complaining and lacking. You decide!

I once worked with a co-worker who would complain about everything. She'd start off with how bad she was feeling. Then she would move on to the way the company did business. Then she'd complain about the weather. It annoyed me that she complained so much about little inconspicuous things all day in the office, but one day she had the nerve to come flop down right at my desk, and start complaining to me. That did it. "Sheila", I told her, "everyday I listen to you complain and I wasn't going to say anything because it's not my business, but now you're sitting at my desk and you're making it my business. No offense, but I really don't want to hear it." Sheila was very offended. As she began to get up from my desk, I asked her to engage in a prayer of thanks giving with me. I told her to lead. She didn't know where to begin. Silently, we sat there for a couple of minutes. She mumbled something. Soon her mumbles turned into an enthusiastic flow of thanks giving.

On average, Sheila would have a pretty crappy day at work. I learned a long time ago that if you're going to work in sales and be successful, you have to have an attitude of gratitude, and you must be faithful. At the time, I was the top producer in the district, and in the top ten in the company. Honestly speaking, that day Sheila out sold me. The next morning she wanted me to lead a prayer of thanksgiving. We alternated prayers of thanksgiving until thanksgiving became Sheila's new attitude.

Exercise: Let's do it! Take a pen and pad and go to town. Write down every single thing that you can think of that you're grateful for. This should be an all day event, so take your list to work with you. All day be sure to be in an attitude of gratitude. When someone does something nice for you, reply immediately with an enthusiastic Thank You! Take note of how you feel, and watch those around you be more inclined to help because of your grateful disposition. Trust me, it works like a charm.

Cool Down: Pray with me: God thank you for a prosperous life. Thank you for everything. I love you, and I appreciate all that I have now. I enthusiastically bless all that is on its way. Thank you, Father, for there is so much to be grateful for. And so it is!

Stretch: Expand your consciousness by working with the word *visualization*.

Day Sixteen: Visualization

What you see is what you get. More importantly, what you see and focus on is what manifests in your life. We have eyes so we're going to see *things* every day. Some images will be attractive to us so we will be likely to hold them in mind. What we are not attracted to, we will dismiss. We will talk more about attraction tomorrow. As for visualization, words such as sight, image, picture, and illusion can be associated with it. I had a friend who had mastered the art of visualization before it even became popular. I watched him unconsciously bring into manifestation all of his hearts desires for years, simply by visualizing.

When I first met him, he was living in a small room in his mother's house. The furniture was pretty worn, and he had a small black and white TV that only played about four channels. In his early twenties, he had some trials and tribulations that set him back a couple of years. Eleven years later, he used those set back as horse power for his personal success. Earning 100 thousand dollars and owning a lavishly furnished two story home was one of his goals. How he was going to do it in the small room in his mother's house, I could not see. But he saw it quite well.

Because of his colorful background, he landed a job as sort of a clean-up guy in a major organization. For the first couple of months, his employer didn't really give him a title. All he knew was that he was supposed to rack and re-rack weights in the weight area and clean the benches and machines. On his job as the "clean up" man, he hung out with the trainers. Watching them train clients daily, he became motivated to get certified as a personal trainer.

In about a month's time, he accumulated more clients than he could count. I know because I was one. Because his schedule was so tight and people still wanted to train with him, they agreed to train in groups. Most of his clients were wealthy and prosperous and had taken a liking to my friend the trainer. They would invite him to exclusive parties and black tie events in their big homes, the kind he would often fantasize about.

He would invite me along to these parties. I would watch him walk around their homes as if their houses belonged to him. He would go in their kitchen unannounced and pour glasses of the finest wine as if he had paid for it. Then he would go from room to room in the rich people's houses with his glass of wine, making himself comfortable in each room. When I'd find him, he'd say one day soon I'm going to live lavishly just like this.

In about six months, he was offered a job as a sales manager of a new location that would be opening in a part of town that was sure to bring in high-end clientele. Without dispute he took it. He took down all of his first place sales reports from the walls of his old, cramped office. The first place sales reports on the wall were a part of his visualization. Within a year and a half, he made over $100,000, and bought his two-story home preconstruction.

My friend hadn't become a millionaire yet but all of his close friends were. He didn't let that stop him from acting and feeling like one. If his friends gave him the keys to their Benzes and Range Rovers, he didn't hesitate to take them for a spin. One of his pals brought him a fancy leather coat, and immediately he put it on and stood in front of a full length mirror for what seemed like hours. When his friends went on vacation, they asked him to house sit, or shall I say, mansion sit.

He became the vice president of sales for one of the biggest personal training companies in the world. That position offered to take his sales ability across the country. Again he didn't hesitate. After closing on three investment properties, he was on the next flight out to Las Vegas. Needless to say, he is worth well over a million dollars today.

Whenever I hear from my friend, he's moving closer to a new vision. He became a millionaire, by mastering visualization. He concentrated on having the desires of his heart and actively pursued them and obtained them before his designated time. Surrounding himself with likeminded individuals and placing himself in positions that were affirmative with his dreams were all a part of his creative process. My friend invested very little time in people and events that would not progressively take him in the direction of his heart's desire. He fertilized his vision with positive thoughts and aggressive action.

So let's sum up visualization. See what you want. Be very specific, making the image of what you want to manifest in your life crystal clear. Praise it, and thank God for it in advance. Spend time around those that are successfully doing what you desire to do. Take action! You may need to change your agenda to spend more time cultivating your dreams. If so, act accordingly. Believe you can have it, and know that you are worthy of it.

Exercise: Take a few moments to become still. As you become still, close your eyes and visualize your heart's desire. When you have done so, take out a pen and pad, and journal about it. At the end of your journaling activity, finish it with, I am worthy to have this and I thank you God in advance.

Cool Down: Pray with me: Lord thank you for perfect vision. I now see my life unfolding harmoniously. As it unfolds, everything that is limiting and negative falls away. Anything I can see, I am entitled to. I only see good for my life. My vision is clear because I see with my mind's eye. And so it is!

Stretch: Expand your consciousness by reflecting on the word *attraction*!

Day Seventeen: Attraction

Take a look around you. What do you see? Who do you see? Chances are you are attracted to that which you see, and that which you see is likely to be attracted to you. We see things just because our eyes are positioned at the top of our face. If we are not attracted to what we see, we simply take notice with a quick glance and continue scooping the scene.

Have you ever been out with a friend to a dance club, or the mall? The two of you can be shopping in the very same department store but you go down totally different aisles and purchase very different merchandise. It wasn't because your friend thought you had horrible taste, it's because you have different interests. In other words, you weren't attracted to the same things.

When I was a teenager, my girlfriend Trish and I used to go out all the time. She would see a guy and say how gorgeous he was then asked me if I agreed. I would stick my finger to the back of my throat as if I was repulsed. When I showed her my *"Mr. Good Looking"* she stuck her finger to the back of her throat to emphasize the same. Trish liked bright color clothing, and hair. She changed her car more times than I changed majors. I was content with a comfy pair of sweats, a white t-shirt, and my black Nissan. Trish wanted to be a real estate agent/fashion model/psychologist/mother of triplet boys. I wanted to teach English to high school kids. Trish and I had nothing in common which is why we both believed our friendship lasted so long. We never stole each other's clothes, or each other's boyfriends.

As we grew older, Trish became a real estate agent, and has her 50th car, (a bright yellow Hummer), and I am writing books. We were not attracted to the same things. You should understand this about attraction. Unlike visualization, where you have to focus on your desire to make it manifest, attraction is quickened by a single thought, and what you are attracted to will eventually show up in your life, whether that was your intention or not. With visualization, you must constantly exercise the desired outcome in mind by seeing it and shaping it the way you want it to appear. When you are attracted to something, it will find you, because it can feel the powerful energy vibrations you send into the universe through thoughts, beliefs, and experiences.

I grew up around men who had been incarcerated. My dad was one of them. I must have been ten or eleven when he asked me what I wanted to be when I grew up. When I told him I wanted to be a prison psychologist, he flipped out. "What makes you want to do something crazy thing like that?", he wanted to know. At ten, I didn't know that I was attracted to the criminal mind, and wanted to study the behavior of a criminal. I just knew that I had paid special attention to my father, uncle, and cousin, and for some reason their behaviors were very interesting to me.

Though my career path changed; my attraction of the male criminal mind followed me for years to come. I got to study the criminal mind first hand often through long in-depth individual case studies. Every man I have ever dated had been incarcerated at some point in his life. There was one who had not been incarcerated but for the past fifteen years, he worked as a correction officer. Three years ago, when I almost married the greatest criminal mind I knew, I made a conscious effort to redirect my attraction. Take inventory of what keeps popping up in your life either consciously or unconsciously. Whether you like it or not, you're probably strongly attracted to it.

Exercise: Answer these questions. What am I attracted to? Does it prosper me? How can I redirect my thoughts to change my attraction toward it?

Cool Down: Affirm: I am the thinker who thinks the thoughts that make the things manifest. Anytime I want to change my surroundings, I can do so by changing my thoughts.

Stretch: Expand your consciousness by meditating on the word *fear*.

Day Eighteen: Fear

Fear is the abortion, and miscarriage, better yet the stillborn birth of anything remotely positive. Emotions characterized by fear, anger, hate, jealousy, pride, shame, and guilt, that go undetected, immobilize the thinker and stunt all healthy growth. Beware; indecision is always near when you are feeling fearful. Some say they are no steel bars locking them up, but if they live in fear, there is no need for bars because fear nails their feet to the ground.

It is easy for some to live in fear, just as it is easy for some to blame God for the discomforts of life. For some, living in fear poses no real challenge. It has become a familiar state of existing for the man who has enslaved himself to fearful emotions. This person knows if they step out of fear, they would have to meet faith, and we all know how challenging it can be to face the situations we'd rather avoid. Faith invites you to check yourself, snatching the covers off and awaking you from a very deep sleep, she gives you the boot so that you can work. This is uncomfortable and unfamiliar for the lazy person hiding behind indecision. We've all come in contact with fear. However, just like the strange man who passes us in the street, we need not engage in a long drawn out conversation with fear, we simply acknowledge it with a firm head nod, and proceed with our plans with faith.

It has been easier for me to assert myself when confronted by fear by understanding its origin. More than often, the negative emotions which are tied to fear derive from an unpleasant experience that we've had in the past. The irresolution of this unpleasant experience still festers within us and when thought about, either consciously or unconsciously, it brings up these hurtful emotions. Overcoming fear is a work in progress, and every time it comes up, we must simply acknowledge it and proceed in faith. Eventually, it will get tired of you giving it the run around.

Exercise: Deny with me: There is nothing for me to fear. At times, situations will appear real; but they are powerless over me unless I fuel them with my energy. I choose to invest my energy in those ideas which prosper me. And so it is.

Cool Down: Affirm: I am courageous and strong. I move forward in love, and love is the strongest force there is. And so it is.

Stretch: Expand your consciousness by reflecting on the word **dependent**.

Day Nineteen: Dependent

Are you dependent? Most of us pride ourselves in being this self made independent person until our faith is tested and we are forced to live without the comfort of our fancy homes, luxury cars, Gucci bags, job title, and sugar daddies. The absence of these material things exposes us, bringing most of us to our knees. This vulnerability shows us where our faith truly lies. We sing songs in church on Sunday, claiming to depend on God for all the desires of our heart, but the minute those things are not present, we become hypocrites. We begin to look outward in a panic, instead of quietly affirming the presence of God and moving in faith knowing that our good will soon appear.

I did not want to be hypocritical so I asked myself what am I dependent on. What I found was that the physical side of me, my ego still has some dependencies. I don't like to admit it because it sounds so "*un-spiritual*" for a *spiritual* person to have dependencies. If I was really *spiritual* I should live like a Buddhist monk or Mother Teresa *right*? Wrong! The truth is the monk and Mother Teresa is no more spiritual than I am. The spiritual level of expression may look different, but that does not mean that they are more spiritual than me. What they did that makes them stick out like blooming daisies in the winter time was give up the dependency of this material world. They proclaimed that they were solely dependent on God or a higher power, and went on to demonstrate that. As a result, they ascended in spiritual consciousness, and this is why they look and behave differently.

Anyway, through a little introspection, I came up with a dependency so trivial that hardly anyone would recognize it. Heck, I almost didn't recognize it. Ready?! I have this thing with my glasses. I have a bad habit of saying I need my glasses to see. Taking this journey with you helped me realize it's not the glasses I'm dependent on. It's the idea of my dependency on them for the sight that God has already given me. Whether my eye sight is 20/20 or not, is not the case. The fact is when

I open my eyes I can see. Some people open their eyes every morning and cannot see. I am blessed with the gift of my vision. So here's what I did. I did away with my glasses for four weeks just to assure myself that my eyesight was not insured by my glasses, but was a gift that God had given me.

To prepare myself for four weeks without my glasses, the first thing I did was go straight to my mirror. I looked myself directly in my eyes and I said, "I see you, and you are beautiful. I see everything clearly and I am so grateful for my gift of vision." Then I went to the local health food market and bought a bunch of organic carrots to juice and crunch on in the process. *Whatever works, right?* I have to admit it wasn't easy driving at night knowing I couldn't be dependent on my glasses. Now don't go running people off the road and then telling the officer that I told you to drive around without your glasses so you wouldn't be dependant. That's my thing. You find yours. Take baby steps. Check to see what you rely on for your good. Behind every dependency, there is an underlying belief that's fear based, whether we want to believe it or not. Like with my vision, I've been working with stepping out on faith. Seeing myself having a prosperous future full of loving relationships makes it easier for me to look forward to the future. So far, I've went from wearing my glasses everyday all day to just wearing them to see the black board when I'm in class, or when I'm driving on the road to unfamiliar places. If I tell you to work on your issues, I'm going to work on my issues too. Remember this; any time you depend on something or someone outside of yourself, you are ignoring God. Basically you're saying to God, excuse me, I think this or that is more powerful than you, or you're saying would you step aside I want him to do it for me; because he looks buff. I'm sure he's stronger than you.

I'll never forget when Hurricane Katrina had come. From what I heard, it was a really bad storm. My family and I were in Atlanta, but we live in Miami. Of course even in Miami we were still blessed compared to New Orleans. My point is this, when we arrived back to our home, things did not look good. In fact, some would say famine had hit the land. I was happy to see that our home was still standing and in tack. Before we could even put our luggage in the house, neighbors had run to our home to tell us of the night of terror. We listened as we moved around the yard picking up roof shingles, and other debris. I realized that whatever comfort I was dependant on in that house I would have to adjust. Sure things like lights, hot water, cool foods would be temporarily unavailable, but what I needed was the AC.

My sisters and I made our way through the dark house which reeked of spoil meat and dead roses. We fondled for the candles in various compartments of the house. One by one, our hands stumbled across them and we began to bring light to an abandoned home. Making our way through the kitchen, we cleared the refrigerator and freezer of whatever was spoiled. That meant everything. My sisters wiped away the foul smell replacing it with lemon Clorox bleach and pine sole. Our house began to look like home again. I left the kitchen to them and walked through our home, which was slowly being rehabilitated. Opening every window, I thanked God that none of them were broken or cracked like the majority of the homes around us.

We spot cleaned everything and the spirit of our house was restored. As much as I didn't like it then, those days of my mother making us crack the windows instead of running the AC sure counteracted the dependency I might have had on it. When my father taught us how to do yard work as women, he empowered us to be able to groom our yard better than most men on the block. In fact, the entire time the power was out, we were the very feminine men on the block. We dragged branches and trees from one block to another while we waited for the garbage men to bring their dump trucks and hall that stuff away. Although I never want to experience anything like that again, reflecting back on it makes me grateful that I was raised to be solely dependent on God.

Exercise: Today is definitely strength training; because it takes a lot of strength to do what you feel you cannot do without. Be totally honest with yourself. What do you feel you can't do without? Whatever that is, go without it today. If you feel the need to do without it longer, by all means, you are the captain of your own mental ship. Whatever it is and it does not have to be tangible either. It could be an idea. Most dependencies are intangible anyway. Our dependencies often lurk in the shadows of those things that we call beliefs. As an exercise for the season of LENT, my congregation had us fast, not from food, but from negative thinking and complaining. In fact, the acronym used for LENT was Lets, Eliminate, Negative, Thinking.

Cool Down: Pray with me: Father thank you for making me aware that everything I need I already have in you, and dare not be dependent on anything or anyone else. Amen.

Stretch: Expand your consciousness with the word ***energy***.

Day Twenty: Energy

There are two primary reasons why a new client seeks my help. The first reason has to do with getting rid of the cellulite in some part of their lower extremities. The second reason is because they want to increase their energy. I hear it over and over again. "I don't know why I feel so tired all the time," they moan. "I hardly do anything during the day. I even take naps; yet I still feel drained." Often times, their faces have impressions of bags underneath both eyes. Their shoulders are usually hunched over. I'll often joke with them, saying you're so tired because you've got the weight of the world on your shoulders.

Already knowing the real cause of the fatigue is the misuse of mental energy I'll still ask the basic questions so I won't totally turn them off from me. Are you eating energy yielding foods, such as an abundance of green vegetables, and juicy fruits like apples and oranges, and staying away from foods that support lethargy such as greasy, fried and processed foods? Are you spacing your foods out over the course of the day to insure that your blood sugar is normal? Are you taking power naps between 30-45 minutes during the day instead of long naps over an hour to make sure that you don't throw off your normal sleep cycle? Are you aware that if you sleep too long during the day and too long during the night frequently that you are forming a dependency on the very behavior of sleep which causes you to feel more lethargic? Are you consuming alcohol? Are you drinking enough water to insure that you're not just dehydrated mistaken it for fatigue? Are you on any antidepressants or other medications that may cause you to feel sleepy? I know that these are a lot of questions, but I ask them to also make you aware of some physical reasons that you too may also be experiencing feelings of energy depletion.

If there is only one thing that I get over to you today this would be it. Even if you experience any of the above, remember this: the number one energy zapper is improper use of mental energy. In my own experience, I have gone days without eating and had more energy than the days I had eaten three balanced meals. On the flip side, I have indulged in cookies and ice cream and still had stamina throughout the course of the day. The energy that you have in you is inexhaustible. Do you know why? Because you have the energy of God in you. Some of you just haven't tapped into it yet.

After I have worked with a client for a while and he is exercising regularly and eating sensibly, if he is still moping around, I only have one question. WHO AND WHAT ARE YOU GIVING YOUR ENERGY TO? I couple that question with this statement: *What do you feel is depleting you?*

Many people don't realize where they are investing or *wasting* their energy. They use their energy like paper plates at a children's birthday party. They give it out to whomever and whatever is willing to use it. All the while, they never replenish themselves, hence feeling depleted. Their energy has now been transferred to all those around them, and even though they have more within them, they feel depleted because of these abrupt transfers. You all remember the charming stranger that Aqueelah helped me escape from, right? Well, looking back I understand why she needed to rescue me. She needed to get me out of there because I was feeling depleted. I was investing all of my time and energy into something that was not feuling me up. Because I was in the midst of pouring my energy out, I could not even think about fueling up. When Aqueelah saw that, she came in and got me out of there. Her telling me to rest was her way of saying fuel up, tap into a new energy source, open your mind and heart and let the energy of God come in you. I must say from that day until now, you'd think I had a shot of B-12 every day.

Here's some good news. If you feel depleted, tired, or drained worry not. Worrying depletes energy. Taking these steps to cultivate a healthier lifestyle will increase your energy no doubt. However for the ultimate jolt of energy get quiet. Ask God to move in and through you and fuel you up with the energy that only He can provide. While the world would have you believe that we are lacking fuel, the fuel that God supply can never be exhausted. Do yourself a favor that's sure to boost your energy. Find the things that give you joy and pleasure and immerse yourself in those things.

I love to workout, read, and write, when I'm doing these things time just goes by and I'm like the energizer bunny with energy reserves, I just keep going and going and going. Find and surround yourself with people who are upbeat and positive. Try not to sit around them with your lips poked out and talk about how hard life is. If you're going to take part in this positive exchange of energy which I think is the very definition of a healthy relationship, at least try and smile and say something optimistic. If you're at an all time low and you can't bring yourself to say anything uplifting just yet, just sit and smile. Sometimes, a smile says more than a hundred empowering words.

Remember you can never get tired when you're working from love. Take some time and find out what you love. What are you passionate about? When you work from passion, you find energy in places you didn't even know existed. I'll never forget the first year I worked for 24 hour fitness. I got to work every morning at 4:30 am. I exercise until 6:30, and I was at my desk at seven. My co-workers and manager could not understand how I could work until ten sometimes eleven at night. The truth is I could have worked around the clock, but I also believe in respecting my body, and while experts say eight hours of sleep will add to better health, me and my body agreed that four to five hours was more than enough. Getting people involved in exercise and fitness really made me feel good. The idea of showing people a new way to live and empowering them to do better for their lives fueled me for a year. I worked most of the time seven days a week, with a four- to five-hour nap.

Exercise: You'll need your pad and pen for this exercise. Answer these questions. What am I passionate about? What will I do if no one paid me to do it? What do I find myself doing without pay just for fun? Once you have answered these questions, find ways to build upon those ideas. You may consider working from them as it relates to your profession, or you might just spend more time doing those things to increase your well-being. You decide.

Cool Down: Affirm with me: "I AM POWER. GOD has given me the energy to do all that he has for me to do. I AM enthusiastic about life and living. And so it is!

Stretch: Expand your consciousness by reflecting on the word ***confidence***.

SUMMER

SUMMER

The Law of Sacrifice

Boy! Oh boy! Oh boy! Oh boy! I can feel the heat! In the same breath, I can feel the breeze too! It's going to be a good summer! I don't know how you feel, but I like a little breeze if I am to tolerate the heat of the summer. I live in Florida so when it gets hot, it gets scorching!

For the summer, we'll be working with The Law of Sacrifice. Now you're starting to sweat. The law of sacrifice is one of my favorite laws. Admittedly, it took me a while to get used to; but now that I am conscious of the way this law works, I must say it is indeed a Law that we abide by whether we are aware of it or not.

Most people don't like the word *sacrifice*. This is because blood is poured on it by traditional preachers in their sermons, and by political authorities who speak of wars. It was because sacrifice was introduced to me this way that I had a problem with the word. That was until I learned its true meaning. When I understood that I did not have to nail myself on a cross, go hungry, and live among the poor, I made peace with the meaning of sacrifice. *To be at peace with sacrifice* sounds scary doesn't it? Don't be scared! Be happy that you have options. God has given you the power to choose. He has given us free will so we can decide what it is that we want to sacrifice and be done with, and what it is that we wish to keep. This is what sacrifice is all about. It simply means choosing to give up something to replace it with something of greater value to you.

Raymond Holliwell says, 'Everything in life has its own price and is always up for sale.' We have to purchase it at the price it demands. Day after day, we go up to life's counter and say. "I will give you this if you give me that." This bartering has another name more familiar perhaps. We call it "sacrifice."

When Holliwell says that everything is up for sale and has a price, most of the time, he isn't referring to money. He is talking about values, morals, and desires. The things that are of less value to us are the things that we readily give up for things that are of higher value to us. Conflict occurs when people start to sacrifice their values, morals and desires, for the desires of someone else. Sacrificing this way is what draws blood and sweat.

Sacrifice works best when you take inventory of yourself and decide what is of lesser value to you that you are willing to give up to receive that which is of greater value. In every act of sacrifice, there will be some loss, but if done consciously, there will also be a continuum of growth. When you sacrifice an hour of your day to exercise, you build a consciousness for prosperity. You sacrificed something, yet you are still growing elsewhere. Since change is inevitable, it would be ideal for us to participate in this transformation by sacrificing those things which no longer serves us for our highest good. Here are two examples of using the Law of Sacrifice. One will bring about promotion and one will nurse stagnation.

Let's go ahead and get the negative one out of the way so we can focus on the positive. I had a classmate who was dating a man for a year. As she articulated her situation, it sounded as if she was in an abusive relationship. The man she was dating was living with her and had not contributed anything financially. He also abused alcohol and had an addiction to marijuana. She expressed her love for the man, and her faith that one day, he would stop abusing alcohol and marijuana and contribute to the household finances. I'm going to stop here because there is something I want to say before we go on. First off, I have learned that you cannot have faith in anyone but God and yourself. You can pray for other people and have faith that *God* will take care of them, but putting your faith in *them* is a waste of energy. I know it might sound harsh, but I felt I needed to say that, because it is our natural instinct, in an attempt to express love for someone, to invest all that we have into them and label it faith or love. I feel we will be more successful if we have faith in God for them, and love ourselves enough to invest our energy in the belief that God can do for others that which He has done for us. Another thing I should mention before we move on is that the act of sacrifice is indeed a personal one.

Sacrifice is not bias. If you put blood and sweat on it, it will operate in blood and sweat. If you put light in its eyes and love in its heart, you can watch it flourish and work for you. You will continue to sacrifice as your consciousness permits. Everyday people make sacrifices that they say are for God. However, their consciousness is ego based, causing them to spiral down. Any sacrifice that is made for God will only lift you up. If it pulls you down, you need to re-evaluate your true reasons for having made the sacrifice.

Now that that's out in the open, back to my classmate. The man she was dating never cleaned up his act and told her that he would not stop smoking because it was a part of his religion. *It's not my business, so don't ask!* The point is the God he served required he smoke marijuana but her God did not agree. She sacrificed her values and her desire to live what she described as a healthy life.

As we went into the next semester, she would often share books with classmates claiming that she could not afford to buy her own. She made a living to support his habit, herself, and now the child that was on the way. That semester she withdrew and she appeared to be very displeased with the decision. I'm not judging her situation. God has brought me out of more than that. I want to show you how easy it is to sacrifice things, values, and ultimately, your soul for a life that you never intended for yourself, and that does not prosper you. When I think of my classmate, I think of a sacrifice that will eventually result in blood and sweat. When we create a life of sacrifices that don't give us the return we want, we create our own hell right here on earth. On the contrary, just like we can create a hell on earth with our sacrifices, we can create heaven here as well. God has given us the freedom to choose.

Let me brighten things up a little! One of the highlights of my career was an elderly couple who had signed up with me at the gym. I met the husband first. He wanted to buy training for him and his wife. I wanted to know where his wife was, since he was the only one at my desk. When he told me that she was in the car because it was too painful for her to walk, I wondered then how she would train. "Let's go and get her," I said. "I would like to at least meet her." He warned me it would be a challenge. I persisted even more. She was sitting in the car parked in a handicap zone. When I saw her face, I couldn't help but smile. Curly jaw length hair fell to her wrinkled rosy cheeks. It looked as if it was somewhat painful for her to smile back, but she managed very well. A cute half grin to the left side of her face gave her eyes a glimpse of hope.

"So your husband tells me you want to work out," I said leaning into the window after she rolled it down. She didn't say anything. She only looked up at me then she shot a perplexed look at her husband still trying to maintain her fading smile.

"Let's get you out of here so you can see the gym," I urged. Her husband reluctantly cooperated and opened the back seat to pull out her walker. As he brought it to the side of the car where she sat, her smile faded away and she began to shake her head as if we had asked her to jump into a swamp of gators. Her husband insisted and because he did, so did I. We gave her encouraging caresses to her shoulders and extended arms for added support. She sucked her fragile teeth, rolled her sea green eyes and grabbed hold to the arm that I had extended. She had a heck of a grip. I had to ask myself if she was holding on, or was she trying to chastise me in some fashion. Her husband looked at me as if to say, *I told you so.*

The walk back to the front door must have taken forever; but patience is a virtue, you learn, when you love what you do. She dug her nails in my arm when she needed to rest to signal me to stop. As we toured the gym, she broke often, holding on to the walls, and rubbing her chronically arthritic knees. Tears filled her eyes when the pain was too much to bear, but they never fell. Her husband looked away when tears began to well in his.

A twenty minute tour took us about a good forty minutes. At this point in my career, I wasn't a trainer, I was a fitness counselor--a fancy title for sales representative. Now, while the membership was sold, that was not enough for me. I explained to them that I would not feel comfortable taking their money if they did not have a trainer. They wanted me to train them but that was not the description of my job title at this time, and I had already been reprimanded for *helping* clients too much. So, I sought out the best trainer for the job. The trainer I chose was patient, funny, and skilled in the water and that was exactly what they would need, because of her diagnosis. To add to that, she had a bulging disk in her lower back. While her husband had similar back injuries, he already claimed his healing and declared he would not live in pain for the rest of his life.

These are the highlights of my career in the fitness industry. The overall experience of empowering people to live healthy and productive lives is what drives me, but cases like this fuel me to be an instrument of empowerment for everyone I meet. This couple made a sacrifice worth mentioning. They were both retired and lived on a fixed income. Her husband worked as a part time pilot to earn extra money for unseen circumstances. Because of their financial situation, I expected them to buy, of course, but I expected them to buy within their *budget*. As they mulled over the plans for what seemed like hours, I was at a loss for words when her husband spent three thousand dollars between the both of them for their membership and personal training.

"I thought you were on a fixed income."

"We are but we're going to sacrifice our yearly trip to New Orleans so that we can get into shape. Next year, when we go, she can leave her walker home."

Denial for Summer

"Pain, sickness, poverty, old age, and death cannot master me, for they are not real." Let's say that again. Pain, sickness, poverty, old age, and death cannot master me, FOR THEY ARE NOT REAL-L-L-L! I realize that's a big vitamin to swallow, but it's one of the ones I take from time to time for that extra boost. Not to worry; it's all natural, straight from the source, so swallow it and wash it down with some purified water.

I know many of us think that the pain in our hip is real. When we see the snot running from our nose, we associate this symptom with a head cold. I know there is a homeless man with a *'will work for food' sign* waving you down at almost every light. When you look in the mirror and see your saggy butt that used to sit up nice and firm, I'm sure you attribute that to aging signs. The 6 feet hole you buried your family member in had to have been real, *right?* I feel you, but even though I feel you I still have to tell you the truth; and the truth is as real as it may seem it is not. *Don't choke! Breathe deeply while I explain.*

Let's take pain and sickness first because our hospital beds are filled with people who are in pain and feel sick. I have a sister who's a nurse, and she never has to worry about a job. Nurses are always in demand. Almost every employer has a medical insurance plan for its employees. I know people who won't even consider a job if the benefits that the employer offers don't include sick leave and medical insurance. Think about that for a minute. The job I chose must afford me the benefit to get sick and take a leave of absence when I get sick, and I also want to make sure they have a plan in my benefits package with insures that I put money away to be sick year round. *Doesn't sound so beneficial, does it?*

I'm going to state the obvious again. GOD IS GOOD ALL THE TIME. This truth statement leaves no room for anything that does not *feel* good, right? *Right.* You are children of the most high right? Right. God doesn't own pain and sickness right? Right. Have you ever caught God screaming from throbbing headache or blowing His nose from congestion? I hope not. If you have, I suggest that you get to know God a little better. Feeling pain in the body and having symptoms of an illness does not mean that you have to own or endure them. You have the power to deny them.

Louise Hayes is the author of Heal Your Life. She is more than qualified to have written a book like that because she cured herself from vaginal cancer. Most all sickness, disease, pain and infection are caused by the way we think and feel. Medical research has shown time and time again that the human body is predisposed for disease. However, as psychologists study mental patterns and disturbances, they have concluded that inaccurate coping strategies of stress is what causes the disease that already lives in the body to malfunction.

Repetitive negative thoughts stress and age our bodies. In more severe cases, what we call death can occur. The good news is none of those things can master you if you learn to master your thoughts. You get sick because you were raised to believe that there is a flu season. Our breast sag because we believe at 30 they are supposed to, and you are comparing your natural breast to someone who has under gone cosmetic surgery. What is old age any way? Heck, today the old twenty is the new forty! If you ever catch me and my mom out and about, you would assume we are sisters, because my mother looks so young.

You must not claim these things to be true for you. Whatever you believe to be true for you at a conscious or unconscious level will become true for you. Negate these things simply by thinking health, wealth and holism. If you were taught to believe that God is a condemning God, then you are more inclined to believe that He made you sick but this is a lie. Good is all good. Never believe He wants anything less than good for you. Here's some food for thought. If you have pain in your body, search your soul to see if emotional turmoil abides. Work on those issues and ask to deliver you from those feelings of pain. Thank Him for His deliverance. Then pay close attention to the way your body responds. Believing you are prone to this, or have the genetic trait for this is one sure way to bring that unwanted experience into physical expression. By now, you should know who your parents are. If you're experiencing any of these things, you need to have a sit down with them. They'll be happy to explain your true family roots.

Affirmation for the Summer

"I am Spirit, perfect, holy, harmonious. Nothing can hurt me or make me sick or afraid. Spirit is God. God cannot be sick, hurt or afraid. I manifest my real self through this body now." All too often, we separate ourselves from God. Yet, in the same breath, we say we are made in His image and in His likeness. We call Him our father, or we say we are spiritual beings, yet we look in the sky instead of looking ourselves in our eyes to connect with God. This may be too powerful for you to believe, but if you have gotten this far, I feel you're ready to hear it. *We are one with God.* We are expressions of God. Everything that God wants done, He uses us to do it. *There is no separation!* We forget that, or we would like to believe that we are these measly little nobodies running around on planet earth having some big bad God in the sky condemn us and put us in bad situations. This is not true.

God has encoded in us the same *gene* that is encoded in Him. He is a powerful God and I AM a powerful Goddess. He is not sick and afraid, and I am healthy, radiant, brave, and courageous. I want you to feel this way about yourself as well. It is easy to believe that you can become sick. You might be sick right now; or you might have just overcome a sickness. *Do you think it was the Tylenol, and the nice doctor at the hospital that made you better?* They may have helped, but the truth is the GOD IN YOU never gets sick; and the GOD IN YOU makes you well and strong. People who recognize the God in them are less likely to get sick, and more likely to recover faster if they do because they are conscious of the power of God that is within.

Have you ever had a pain in a certain part of your body that aggravated you all day long, then you woke up the next morning and it was gone? That was the God in you. Have you ever had a fear of something and one day you just walked up to the thing you feared looked it in the eye, and said I am not afraid? That was the God in you.

People often looked startled when they ask me how I'm doing and I declare, *excellent and striving for perfection*. I respond that way because, first of all, that's the way I feel. Second, I know that God and I are one; and if God is perfect, then I have the potential to be perfect too. Excellence is very close to perfection. I rationalize it this way. When I was ignorant of my oneness with God, my life was fair. When I at least knew I could talk to Him and He'd respond, some of the time I did good; but the day I called for Him, and He responded, *I AM HERE, RIGHT IN YOU,* joy filled up in my heart, and suddenly I became excellent. *I can't wait to see what the future holds for us*!

Take Home Sample Work Out for Summer

Exercise: Inhale slowly through your nose and breath out even slower as you blow out through your mouth. Deny with me, in silence three times: Pain sickness, poverty, old age, and death cannot master me, for they are not real.

Cool Down: Pray with me. Lord God, if I ever believe that you were not accessible to me, I forgive myself now. Now that we are together, we shall never part, and so it is.

Stretch: Expand your consciousness by meditating on the word **indecision**.

Day Twenty-One: Indecision

Having the ability to make a decision and stand by that decision is the foundation of an accomplished life. When you decide on something, no matter how difficult it seems, you are taking ownership of your life. Far too often, people are indecisive, and wishy washy about life. The person who can't make decisions for him or herself is really saying I don't think I can do it. I don't know if I'm worthy. My confidence is faulty. The person who is indecisive does not realize the God in them. I can go on to say that the person who is indecisive is weak in faith.

Now, I'm not trying to be hard on you. I understand that some decisions call for a little more time. However, if you find yourself at a standstill, when it comes to deciding on something, make sure that you are not procrastinating. Procrastination will keep you out of the flow, and this is a sure way to miss an increase or a raise from God.

I had a trainer once whose favorite motivational line was, "*make a decision*"! When my body got to a sticking point during one of our training sessions and I believed I could not push out any more reps, he would assume spotting position to insure that I did not hurt myself. Then he would get close to my ear and he would command me, "MAKE A DECISION"! He would ask, "*are you going to dig deep and get the results you want or are you going to give up because you're a little uncomfortable.*" Anytime I heard those words, I realized it was time to make a decision. I realized my progress depended on it. I could either stay where I was, or I could achieve more results. Every time my trainer commanded that I make a decision, I often doubled what he ask for. He always stood up straight, crossed his arms over his chest, looked me in my eyes, and smiled. "Good *decision, you'll be happy with your results.*"

Most people don't know that indecision or indecisiveness is the antagonist of success. Indecisiveness feeds procrastination and stagnation. Fear thrives in the mind of the person that is incapable of making a decision. People who cannot make decisions on their own don't trust themselves. I once heard someone say if there is no trust then there is no love. So I ask you, do you love yourself enough to trust that you can make your own right decisions? Key words to think about *your* and *own*.

Many people go around asking others what they should do with the life that God gave them. It is important to me that you understand and believe what I am about to tell you. God will support any decision that you make for your own life as long as your heart is pure, and your intention is good. Why else do you think He gave us free will? Do you think He gave each of us free will so that we may give our freedom to choose to someone who has the same ability to think just as we do?

When you go calling up all of your friends and folks that you think have more sense than you, asking them what they think you should do with your life, you're discrediting yourself, and not trusting God. What you're really saying is, "*here my life is in your hands. I can't think for myself. I don't trust or value my relationship with God to support me.*" This may sound bad, but many people think this way. They are too afraid or lazy to think for themselves so they leave the work to someone else. I listen to people talk smack about Michael Jackson, but he knew something that others did not know when he made that song about the man in the mirror. He understood early on that in order to change you must first look within.

Realize that when you have others make decisions for you, the down side to that is you're basing you're life on someone else's bias, opinions, views, and experiences. You're ruling out the option to create a life founded in the purity of your own imagination.

Whether the decisions that you make are right or wrong is not the issue. The point is practicing decision making enables you to think for yourself. It builds your self-confidence and self-esteem. I can't tell you how many times I asked someone for their advice, until one day, God spoke in my heart and I've been quiet ever since.

Here's something else to consider. People won't mind if you come to vent and seek advice the first couple of times. However, if you insist on these behaviors, they'll become agitated with you; and no matter how much they love you, what they'll be saying to themselves and others is, "I wish that poor child gets it together." When they see your phone number on the caller ID, they may start to let their answering service pick up more often.

I have a friend who lives in Atlanta who I can't help but admire. This girl will make a decision so quick it would make your head spin. I respect her though because every choice she makes, good or not so good, she owns up to it and she's not afraid to make another, regardless of the results of the previous decision. Now, while I do believe in proceeding with a little more caution than my friend, I have to admit growing up around her enabled me to see that even bad decisions can be severed just as long as you stop making them.

Exercise: Affirm with me: I am an excellent decision maker. All of my decisions prosper my life. I am confident that every decision I make is supported and uplifted by the Lord.

Cool Down: Affirm with me: Making right decisions for my life is as easy as swallowing water. I am a master decision maker. Like the water I ingest, I know every decision I make for myself will help me grow healthy and strong. For it is not the outcome that concerns me, it is the journey that my decision takes me on which allows me to grow and unfold. In this knowing I am confident that my best life is on its way. I trust myself, because I love myself. I love myself as I exercise my God given right to chose. There is no need to rely on the opinions of others. I lift my own weight. I watch in delight as I grow beautiful healthy muscle. I think right. I choose right. I make the best decisions for a life of prosperity. And so it is!

Stretch: Expand your consciousness by meditating on the word ***confidence***.

Day Twenty-Two: Confidence

Webster's dictionary describes CONFIDENCE as a positive feeling arising from an appreciation of one's own abilities; self-assurance. Here's a story that tested my own confidence. Four years ago, I managed a personal training department in a small all women health club. I loved that place. The interpersonal relationships that I established with women of all ethnicity really brought me joy and fulfillment.

There was one woman by the name of Nikki. Nikki wanted me to train her six months into her pregnancy. She wanted to have a healthy pregnancy, and felt training would decrease her chances of weight gain, and prompt a smoother delivery. From what I understood about exercise and pregnancy, she was right. Honestly speaking, something about training a pregnant woman made me a little apprehensive. If I decided to take her on as a client, she would be my very first pregnant client. Of course, I had trained women pre and post pregnancy, but I never dealt with a mother and her unborn child at once. The thought of it made me apprehensive *yes*, but the idea of a *successful* outcome had my eye brows raised.

What if I trained Nikki and she delivered a healthy baby, gained more health in the process, *and* lost all of her baby fat after she had given birth. This would be a true accomplishment for me, and it would definitely boost my confidence as a trainer! Nikki told me how much weight she gained from her first pregnancy. She also told me that her husband was not pleased about her not doing much to lose the weight. When she expressed that she no longer looked at herself in the mirror, tears began to roll down Nikki's cheeks. At this point, I knew I was going to train her. Something came over me that only God could stop, and before I knew it, I had committed to training a six-month pregnant woman who looked all of nine. *What was I thinking? What had I just gotten myself into?*

I did not want to be dishonest with Nikki by withholding that piece of information, so I told her straight forward. "Nikki, you are so blessed and lucky", I said with my hands folded in front of me and a huge cool-aid smile. "I am?" she replied, looking somewhat confused. "Yes, you are blessed and you are blessing me because you are my first pregnant client. *Ever*! I am going to take my time training you so that you can have a healthy strong house for your unborn child." I rubbed Nikki's stomach. "What are you having anyway?"

"I don't know yet and I won't know until the birthday." I'm not sure if it was my apprehension or not, but after I told Nikki that I had never trained a pregnant woman, she looked nervous, but she tried hard to hide it. So I did the same.

"Okay, whoever you are, we're going to be seeing a lot of each other, so let me introduce myself. My name is Nadirah." As I spoke into Nikki stomach, she tried to smile. She then confirmed that she'll be back with the check next week Friday. She wanted to wait until pay day and talk it over with her husband. While I was not always happy about waiting on money from a client, Nikki's case was an exception. I was actually happy that she didn't want to train right away. This would afford me enough time to collect every magazine on healthy pregnancies there was and go over the *very vague* material they had given me in my certification text.

When I saw Nikki on Friday, she came in with a smile so big she lit up the place. "How are you, Nikki," I smiled back. "How are you little Nikki or Nicholas?" I asked rubbing her stomach. Nikki smiled bigger. She sat at my desk and I explained to her the procedures and how things would go. In agreement, she wrote her check. Before she handed me the check, she handed me an envelope. I tore it open as I watched Nikki's eyes lower and her smile fade away. That got me nervous again, but I kept my smile big and my mind on her and her baby's successful outcome. The letter was from her husband it read: *I am confident that you will not hurt my wife and you will take extra care of my unborn child.*

Thank you for your services. Nikki seems to like you, so I have no choice. My smile was kind of fixed on my face and for some reason it felt kind of tight, and uncomfortable. *Be confident I told myself. You are capable of doing this. Just remember what you studied and go for it.* So I did.

"Your husband really loves you huh Nikki?" She nodded in agreement. "That's great and I am honored that you all have as much confidence in me as I have in myself. We're going to work well together." Nikki's smile came back and I got to work. To say the least, I worked with Nikki up until her last month of pregnancy. She gave birth to a healthy seven and a half pound baby boy, and returned to train with me four weeks after her delivery. I guess she had confidence in me. I know one thing Nikki would have never had confidence in me if I hadn't had confidence in myself. *By the way, her husband paid for her resign.* I guess it's safe to say it pays to be confident.

Exercise: Answer these questions. What area in my life could I apply a little confidence? What have I wanted to do, but have not done because I've been feeling a little nervous? As you think about and come up with a response to those questions, take time to sit quietly and imagine yourself doing it in pure confidence. As you sit quietly, make sure that your shoulders are square, your navel is pulled in and your chin is high. This is a confident position. Imagine yourself successfully completing all that you desire to do. When you are done, before you open your eyes, affirm, "And so it is!"

Cool Down: Affirm with me: I AM CONFIDENT IN THE LORD. GOD IS ALWAYS WITH ME. WITH HIM, I SHALL NOT FAIL. Repeat ten times.

Stretch: Expand your consciousness with the word ***word***.

Day Twenty-Three: Words

In case you hadn't noticed, the entire purpose of this book is to motivate, empower, and expand your awareness so that you can live from wholeness. I would not be able to carry out this mission if I were at a loss for words. Many of us don't even realize the power that is in the things we say. The words we use shape and form everything we see outside of us. It is important to be sure that the words that come from our mouths are uplifting to ourselves and others.

Coming up, my mother had a rule for us. Her rule was no name calling. I broke that rule coming up a couple times, and when I did, let's just say it wasn't pretty. I'll never forget, I had a math teacher in the sixth or seventh grade, named Ms. Smith. Ms. Smith was old and mean. That is the only way I could remember her. While I don't believe in being too old to do anything, Ms. Smith *acted* very old. Her beliefs and attitude were old and outdated, causing her to speak very harshly to her students. She often yelled and screamed, and called us stupid. She would even slap the boys on the back of their heads with her note pad. That wasn't legal in the public school system but everyone, including me, was too scared to tell anyone.

Unfortunately Ms. Smith had to teach me pre-algebra. This was a very challenging subject for me to grasp back then. One day, I really needed some help solving an equation. Reluctantly, I raised my hand to ask Ms. Smith if she could help me. The woman had the audacity to call me stupid in front of the whole class, including Jimmy, who I had a major crush on. Jimmy was a math whiz, and he was the one boy in the sixth grade that I could ask for help who would not call me booty lips. I could not ask Jimmy for help, because every time I did, Ms. Smith would tell me to shut my big mouth and stop being fresh. I was forced to risk being embarrassed in front of the class when I raised my hand. After that day, I never asked a question in her class again.

I passed junior high, but in high school, I failed pre-algebra, because I'd cut that class, or sit in my chair and wouldn't ask a question to save my life. Later on, I had trouble in Algebra, and when it was time to graduate, I almost did not receive my diploma because I could not pass the math portion of the High School Competency Test. It's funny because I was an honors student in all other subjects. I was voted Homecoming Queen, and had been elected to hold office in many of my high schools clubs and organizations. Authorities believed I had a learning disability in mathematics. Now that I understand how words can shape people, I realize that my struggles in math were a result of the way Ms. Smith used to talk to her students. The words we use daily have the ability to empower—or to diminish power.

"The Word became flesh, and dwelt among us." (John 1:14) Ask yourself do you want to be confronted with love, peace, harmony, and empowerment, or do you want to live amongst stupidity, ugliness, hatred, and jealousy? Ever heard the expression *"one day you will have to eat your words"*? There you have it! I don't know about you, but even though I eat healthy I still like things that taste good. Speak right, using words that uplift and empower you and those around you. This way you will always add sweetness to your recipe of life. .

The next time you want to curse someone out, or tell someone off, try hard to keep your lips together, and avoid saying something that may potentially leave a scar forever. Let's not belittle ourselves and each other by using harmful words. I'd like to make one more point before wrapping up this exercise. The thoughts you think in the quiet of your mind are still made up of words. Just because you don't say it out loud doesn't mean they were not said. Having said that, beware of negative self-talk.

Exercise: Today, I'm going to ask that you to fast. Don't worry, you can eat. However, today you will be fasting from speaking any words of condemnation, envy, hate, judgment, guilt, and the like. It will require that some of you actually spend the day in silence, since most of your ill talk goes on in your mind. You will have to consciously reframe and reform your thoughts into positive words of affirmation.

For the rest of the day, only speak words of good report. If you feel that you need to tell your boss off today, reframe from that. If you feel the need to straighten someone out, let it pass. I'll bet you ten bucks, the urgency will not be there tomorrow. This will be a challenge, but by now you all should have built up enough muscle to be able to carry out this exercise. All day today, if you begin to criticize yourself mentally or verbally, kiss yourself on the hand like the prince does the princess and softly say to yourself, "Those words are not true, and I love you and encourage you." Practice this all day. When I did this exercise myself, people thought I was narcissistic. In class, I was kissing my hand. At the gym, I was kissing my hand. I would wake up in my sleep and kiss my hand. Let's just say I was doing a lot of washing and kissing my hand.

Cool Down: Pray with me: God, thank you for letting me use my words to uplift and empower. Thank you for letting my words harmonize and heal. I now use the power of spoken words right in my life, and so it is.

Stretch: Expand you consciousness, by reflecting on the word **will**.

Day Twenty-Four: Will

If you did the exercise right yesterday, then the back of your hand probably still has your lipstick on it. Today, I'm giving you permission to go ahead and flex those beautifully toned muscles; because today my friend it's all about WILL. Will and I have had a great relationship since grade school. In grade school, I didn't know what to call him. I just knew he was around when I would do the things I thought I was too afraid to do. Whenever Will was around, I would have to get out of my comfort zone, roll up my sleeves, and strap up my boots. I'd walk through the fire with Will by my side and, somehow, I never got burned.

Do you have a pal like Will? I think you might. Sometimes, we identify him as Determinism, Faith, Courage, or Tenacity. I call Will the big brother in the family. He's responsible, yet strong, he's accomplished and serious. Will gets the job done when no one else in the family wants to do anything. He takes initiative. He's the motivator. He's the hero that'll pull a stranger to safety. I believe I met Will that night when mommy and daddy tried to keep me caged in the dungeon at the gym. Will dragged me out of there. I never had a big brother. In fact, I'm the oldest of my mom and dad's four children, but sometimes, the oldest needs a little direction too. So I created a big brother in Will.

Will is also responsible for character formation and spiritual growth. So is it safe to say that if there is no will, a person may stunt his or her spiritual growth? I believe this is true! Here's why! The last line of this definition supports my claim. "When man wills to do the will of God, he exercises his individual will in wisdom, love, and spiritual understanding; he builds spiritual character." Now, if you've been listening to my story, you would have heard that my passion for fitness started for me when I was very young. I loved weights, treadmills, and trampolines, before I knew how to spell them. Although, I did not understand at the time that people were exercising to lose weight and tone up. Intuitively, I knew that their emotional well-being was connected to the physical act we call exercise. Maybe it was because my mom and dad came back from the gym all smiles. Maybe it was the trips as a family that we'd take to the whole food market after their workouts for smoothies and fresh carrot and beet juice, maybe it was my own euphoric feeling that welled up inside of me just watching my mother in an aerobic class. Who knows? The fact is I have grown spiritually in the fitness industry. I have also built moral and disciplined character.

Charles Fillmore says that Will can be thought of as a man who has directive power and helps form character. If there is something that you would like to see manifest in the physical form, you must not give up when you are faced with adversity. You must press on using faith, wisdom, and courage to take you to your destination. This reminds me of the mantra, "Anything worth having is worth working for and waiting for." I think Will made that up!

I must have gotten my will from my father, because he is one man who sets his eye on something and he goes for it full fledge. I remember my senior year in high school my dad declared that he would receive his high school diploma in the form of his GED. My father was an academic disciplinarian. When I say disciplinarian, I say that with a capital D! My father spent money on math games, vocabulary books, spelling books, chalk boards, flash cards, you name it we had it. He didn't buy that stuff so it would look pretty on our toy shelves either. He bought it, and we were required to use it. Our teacher taught us in school, and they gave us a test, but my father and mother didn't leave it to them to make sure we understood the lesson. While daddy was at work, mommy made sure we learned our timetables and vocabulary. I could still hear that lady singing the timetable song. She was so aggravating; because she was so happy, and I was so frustrated trying to keep up with her. Anyway, when daddy got home from work he put his work bag down, pulled up a chair to the dining room table, and called us out. I was always first because I was the oldest. *Nadirah! Jihad! Aaliyah!* One by one we tipped toed to the dining room table, while my baby sister Zakiyyah crawled under the table to watch.

Daddy held up the flash cards and it was on and popping; and I do mean popping if we didn't know those times tables. I may have gotten one or two pops, but it was all good because when it was time for vocabulary and spelling words, I got money. Ten dollars for every word I spelled right and used in a sentence. By the time I had finished receiving my money, I didn't even feel my backside throbbing. Sometimes, I walked away with all of daddy's tip money. Mommy was taking some child care classes at Miami-Dade Community College, so now she was learning that spanking wasn't so good. This was great! She told daddy there would be no more spanking only rewarding and taking away things of value. So, the next time daddy pulled up the chair to the kitchen table, we only got money, and if I didn't do good on my times tables, he subtracted five dollars for every times table I missed from the money I earned for my spelling words and vocabulary. To be honest that was a better strategy, because when I realized I wouldn't be able to go to the flea market and buy that gold-plated rope chain I was saving up for, I learned those times tables in order and out of order. I couldn't have my old man cutting in on my profit. *Hey, what can I say it was a good way to learn adding and subtracting in the triple digits!*

I realized later that my dad was studying with us. He was also insuring our education. His will for us to be successful in academics inspired him to get his GED. It took him about two years, because he had trouble in English. He would bring his essays home and have me check them for grammatical errors. It's so funny because when I had trouble in math in college, my father's will resonated in me again. At 24 years of age, I was still having trouble in algebra so I walked right into Sylvan's Learning Center with my mom to hire a math tutor. Could you imagine at 24 I had 12 year olds helping me break down algebraic equations? All because I had the will to learn. It's ironic because prior to that my father went to the same center at 30+ to get tutored in English. Talk about Will.

Exercise: Pray with me: Lord God, let your will in my life be done. Amen.

Cool Down: Affirm: I have the will to accomplish the things that I want to do in my life NOW! Repeat 10 times.

Stretch: Expand your consciousness by meditating on the word **rest**.

Day Twenty-Five: Rest

How are you today my grace? If you've been using *will,* I'm sure you could use some rest. So today should be fairly easy. For those of you who are use to a constant state of arousal, this may be a challenge. As I see it, most Americans seem to find it difficult to just *chill.* If it's not the house phone, it's the cell phone. If it's not the cell phone, it's the urgent email coming in from your boss by way of cell phone. Do you know that right now in Florida most car accidents are a result of text messaging? What kind of message can be so important that you would jeopardize your life or the life of someone else?

I have a friend who just went out and bought some kind of phone that looks like a mini-radio with an antenna that goes up, so she can do something with a iPhone, and eat a blackberry, to get a different ring tone for everyone who calls, so she can check her emails, with blue teeth, and talk to her boss at the same time while she runs on the treadmill. *Don't ask!* I haven't a clue. People have been telling me to upgrade my phone since I got it. I get my calls. I make calls, and that's that.

I could never understand how I see some people go for weeks, months, years, even decades without stopping for a few moments of silence. They only stop to sleep, and even then, their wheels are turning faster than the tires on a Ferrari. I don't know about you, but when I use to ignore my mind when it told me to stop, my body would begin to speak to me. We all know that we could ignore the mind all we want, but when the body starts to yell *migraine,* or *chest pain, ulcers,* that's when we call our managers and say we need time off. Let's not wait until it becomes so drastic. Last night in my stress management class, I learned that almost all gastro intestinal problems are a derivative of stress. Things like high blood pressure, aneurisms, and most back pain are plaguing people because they refuse to sit down for thirty minutes out of their day to reconnect themselves to God. Trust me, I know what a hectic schedule looks like, but even with a hectic schedule, it is crucial to take time out, and even more so. We believe that because our agenda is so chaotic that we have to rip and run faster than Marion Jones to meet the *demands* of our daily lives. In the morning, you run the kids to school. Then you run to the grocery store. Then you run to work. Then you run errands for your boss. Then you run to pick up dinner. Then you run to your husband at the end of the night. My friend, that is a lot of running. You'd think with all that running, you'd have the perfect waistline and your doctor would have reports that you are in your best health, but you and I know that that's not the case.

The fact is you're struggling to keep your waistline down and you're taking medication for high blood pressure because you failed to include one thing in your busy schedule. Rest! Running is my favorite form of exercise. I love to run; but when my body says, "Nadirah I want to stop running for a while." I take off the new balances, and put them away for days, weeks, and sometimes months, depending on the signal I get from my body.

Speaking from a fitness stand point, the same concept for our mental well-being holds true for our physical well-being. The body can only repair itself after you stop working it. When you weight train, you tear down muscle or bruise it badly. In order for it to heal, you have to replenish it, and rest. Have you ever tried to run and eat? What kind of question is that? Of course you have, especially if you live in America. The question is how many times have you spilled your coffee on your shirt, or choked on the hot dog you were trying to scarf down before you went into the courthouse. Some of you have developed acid reflux disease from that very action. Try this. The next time you eat, sit down and chew your food, bite by bite. Swallow only what you've fully masticated. If you do this properly, you should not have to gulp as the food goes down your throat. It should be a very easy process. When you've completed your meal, just sit for about ten minutes before you drink anything. Then sit for another ten minutes as you feel the digestion process taking place. This is not only healthy for your digestive system, it is also healthy for the mind. It takes your mind off everything else you are pressed to do and it puts you in the moment, which is the healthiest place for your mental well-being.

I used to have a roommate who used to read the newspaper while she ate breakfast. It never failed for her to either knock over her plate or coffee. If she didn't knock over her food, she would just rant and rave about the economy, the crime, the *stupid president* or whatever else she was reading about. The point is she never enjoyed breakfast, because she was everywhere but the breakfast table. Every single day, except Sundays, she would start her day off like this, and every day, she experienced one unfortunate event after the next. When I suggested maybe she read the paper after breakfast, she told me she needed to be informed about current events before she started her day.

I had a client who was obsessed with losing weight. I gave her a routine to follow which consisted of a three day a week weight training, two days of cardiovascular training, and two days off. You know this woman did not listen to me. I knew she didn't listen because when I was working out on my day off, I saw her in the gym going to town. Her explanation was she was trying to burn of a slice of cheesecake. Cheesecake or no cheesecake on your rest days you must *rest*. Do your extra thirty or forty five minutes on your workout days. Either way your body will respond the same as long as you incorporate the extra time in the gym on any given day. She ended up losing very minimal weight because she had her body in a constant state of stress. There was no time to rest. After she worked out, she wanted to hit the club. After she hit the club, she had to go to the mall. After the mall, she was back at work. It went on and on and on until she gained back every pound she lost and more. When she came back to pay for more sessions, I told her I would love to train her if she could just take two days off, away from everything and just rest. She couldn't do it. The next day she was back at it again. I referred her to another trainer.

This piece of advice is for you. Even in your greatest efforts, don't forget to give yourself time to breathe. In other words, don't forget to rest voluntarily. When you fail to take initiative and rest voluntarily, what happens is the universe has ways of making you rest whether it was on your agenda or not. It could be through a tragic accident, which leaves you disabled. Then you don't have a choice but to sit down and take care of yourself. It could be that you get laid off from your job or a child may get sick forcing you to spend more time at home. It may sound weird, but pay close attention to the events in your life. Situations arise in our lives to create balance where it is lacking. God made it so that everything in creation has time to rest including Him. Although I believe you are great, you are not an exception.

Exercise: Today, I want you to rest. If you have a billion things to do today that cannot wait, fine. You should try to incorporate this day into your schedule as soon as possible. If you already have time off or you're a stay at home mom, great. Even if you work today that's still great. My intention is not to pull you away from your daily activity. It is to slow you down. I want you to try and release the anxiety that often comes with trying to get everything done in a perfect manner.

When you're in traffic today and the kids are thirty seconds away from being late, don't start honking the horn in a frenzy, just sit there in your car, turn the radio off, take two or three deep breaths and just *know*, that everything is fine even though it may not look that way. Today, if your boss storms into your office and throws a pile of files onto your desk, don't curse her out in your mind. She can't hear you so you're only stressing and cursing out yourself. Simply smile at her, take a deep breath, and bless her on her way out of your office. When she turns her back, simply put the new stack of files out of visual sight until you have completed the files you were working on.

Remember, God doesn't place a burden on us greater than we have the strength to bare. I can go further than that and say God doesn't place a burden on us at all. We make a very light load burdensome when we place demands on ourselves or when we measure our self worth and the efficacy of our daily lives. When the load gets heavy, check to be sure you are not too anxious.

Remember the people we try and please, such as your boss, had to work as hard as you are working now to attain that position. So why be mad, and why stress out. Simply do your work and have fun doing it. If you're at a job you hate, I understand that can be stressful but guess what, God has blessed you with gifts and talents so that you can be your own boss. So start to make changes. Your future is not in the hands of your manager. Your future is in your own hands. If your hands are always in a fist because you're mad and stressed out, you're choking the life out of what can be a very promising future.

Also for those of you who are at home, try taking a nap today for about 30-45 minutes. If you're at work, do yourself a favor and really take a break. This means tell your lunch crew that today you want to do lunch alone. When you take your break today, find somewhere quiet for you to just sit and listen to nature or your own breathing. If you insist that you can't find a quiet space, go in your car and listen to some smooth jazz or new age. Whatever you do, don't listen to the news, and don't run errands. Just sit there and relax until your break is up. Use this time to pray and commune with God. I guarantee when you go back to work, your body will be carrying out the task, but the flow of energy that you have introduced yourself to will now set the tone for peace that will be around you for the rest of the day, making your task a breeze and your boss appear to be a little spoiled child. Try it! You can thank me later.

Cool Down: Take several deep breaths. Affirm and deny with me: I am at peace. Right here right now I am at peace. I cannot be disturbed no matter what is going on around me, peace is still in me. My energy is good and easy. My breathing feels good. As I inhale, the luscious air of life, and exhale all that is frantic, all that is urgent, all that is negative. I inhale love. I inhale peace. I inhale joy. My energy is good. My energy is wonderful, because my life is wonderful. I am capable and willing to live a life of peace. I am not disturbed by outer appearances and circumstances because I know the truth. I accept the truth. PEACE BE STILL. Peace be so still in me, so that my world is peaceful. And so it is.

Stretch: Expand your consciousness by meditating on the word ***music***.

Day Twenty-Six: Music

What did you wake up to this morning? Did you wake up to your alarm clock? Did you wake up to your dog licking you in the face? Did you wake up to your significant other whispering I love you in your ear? Did you wake up to your kids pounding down your door because you overslept and they were late for school? What is the first thing you hear when you wake up in the morning? What is it that you hear continually throughout the day? Whatever it is that's your *music.* That's the beat that you dance to whether you like what you're hearing or not. Anything that gets you moving and keeps you moving is your beat, and your action to what is being said is your dance. Some people go their whole lives dancing to the same beat and singing the same songs that they claim they dislike. Yet, they never switch the beat, and they never change the words to the song. They just dance. Some of them have no rhythm, while others connect so deeply with the music, they play it as if they were in a ballroom all by themselves getting down and sweaty, shaking a tambourine in their hand while slapping their knees with the other. This is the person who enjoys life because they have studied the music of the world. They have thrown out the albums they did not like while keeping the ones that they did. They are true artist, creators, and lyrical geniuses. After listening to the same old tired hum drum chorus, they decided to re-write their own song, and now weather the folks around them are dancing or standing on the wall they are always on the move because they got their music.

These are the folks that can hold a note. These are the people who can dance by themselves and still look good, or they can dance with a partner and not smash his toes. These folks can blend in with a group, and can still be recognized as an individual. They understand that it's sometimes necessary to work in a band, so co-existing is easy for them.

One summer, I took an African dance class because my baby sister kept telling me I had no moves on the dance floor. It was fun, and let's just say, I did better than I thought I would do. I danced with the class and I even helped some of my classmates learn the steps to the *mambo!* I danced salsa with my partner and his feet are just fine. For our final project, I had to finish a solo act. I earned a B+. According to the teacher, I needed to be sure my music was on point if I wanted to earn an A.

We don't realize that we sing a song every day. Words that we consistently use are our own personal song. Have you ever talked to a person about a situation or circumstance, and realized that you could finish their sentence before they even opened their mouth? If so, you have memorized their song. I had a co-worker, and you can rest assured knowing that if you ask her how her day was going she would sing, "S.O.S." (*same-old...you can figure out the rest*) Her tone would be the same. The pitch would be the same. So I called that her chorus, because that was the line that she was guaranteed to throw in, throughout the whole conversation. If you asked her anything else, she would highlight every health problem, or another debate she had with management. She moved around the office holding her hip. Her beat was a little off so she walked with a limp, but that was her dance. She loved the Blues. No matter how popular the Blues may have been, that's just music that I simply can't get with.

On another note, I have a friend who I love to be around. I invite him everywhere because he brings life to the party. With him, you never know what he's going to say, but you know it's going to be something positive. When my sisters and I invited him to a party and things didn't always go as planned, he was the one who'd say, "It's all good; we can still have a good time," and boy, could he dance. He'd dance with the ladies. He'd dance by himself, or he'd dance in the group doing the electric slide. It didn't matter what they played because the man had his own beat, and he was always in rhythm. That was a man who really knew music, and fully enjoyed the beat of life. If more people could sing and dance like him, our world would be a party within a party.

Exercise: *Make Music!* That's right, I said make music! I don't care if you're not the artsy type, or you're more into computers or politics, I'm asking you to take time to make some music. I'm no musician, but I'm going to help you with what I know. Now I know we need a beat, a tune or melody, and some words, at least a chorus. So, grab your pad and pen.

The Beat: The beat is the thing that you tap your feet to, or you bop your head to. So we'll call the beat the *feeling*. Right now, find a seat and began to tap your feet, and bop your head. Don't worry about people looking at you because they need to appreciate music also. Now that I got you moving a bit, you should feel good. Whatever that good feeling is, stay with it. Now close your eyes. What are you thinking about? Are you thinking about health, money, love, good relationships? Whatever it is, write it down. Okay, good. You're going to need this beat to carry you home. So remember this feeling. That's your beat.

The Chorus: The chorus has to be something you can always say to bring you back home. It's your center. It's the place you go when you have nothing else to say. Okay, got it? Good! The chorus will be our positive thoughts. Alright! I don't know about you, but I'm really beginning to like making music.

The Song: Plan and simple, the song are the words. Now the words we put out are a reflection of our thoughts and our thoughts are directed by our feelings. Doesn't this sound harmonic? Okay, are you ready to sing and dance? I'll share with you a piece of my song. I don't know if this is rap, or spoken word or whatever! One thing I do know. I know it's not the blues! So here we go!

> *"One. One two. One. One two three.*
>
> *I'm sitting here contemplating on the goodness of God,*
>
> *And it feels so natural, not the slightest bit odd,*

Maybe it's because God is a part of me,

Thinking of His grace gets me weak in the knees,

I'm a child of the most powerful king,

I'm rich and wealthy and I don't want for anything,

I'm PERFECT. I'M WHOLE and I'm COMPLETE. You need to get like me, you need to get like me.

I say one. One two. I say one. One two three. You need to get like me. You need   to get like me.

I'm connected to the source,

Yes of course,

By my father God I am endorsed,

I got money in the bank,

And God I thank,

For Him giving me heaven right here on this earth,

Man oh man talk about a rebirth.

I say one. One two. I say one. One two three. You need to get like me, you need to get like me. Perfect Whole, and so complete.

Even in my imperfection, I'm still perfect,

Don't try to get on my nerves cause I won't let one work it,

I love myself and that's a fact,

If you want to rain on my parade, you best step back,

Because I'm going to still march high in the name of the lord,

Holding up truth, not a shield and sword,

I say one. One two. I say one. One two three. You need to get like me. You need   to get like me. Perfect whole, and so complete.

Boy oh boy! I think I'm going to try my hand at inspirational rapping. What do you think? You get the point. Every morning, you should wake up to your own song.   The music that you make for yourself should be motivating, inspiring, and loving, and you need to dance to that all day long even when times get tough.

Cool Down: Pray with me: Lord God I realize that you have given me power so that I can bring the things that I want in this life into fruition. I understand that the power of my tongue plays an important role in my creative process. Lord God, I wish to create after the ideas that are like you. Lord God, make my demeanor a pleasant one. Make my eyes and mouth bless and not criticize and scold. Let my ears hear your melody, and let my body respond in accordance by always dancing to the rhythm that you provide. Lord God, I understand and I thank you for the part that I play in the harmonic tune of the world. Bless me to always be a key. In this I pray, and it is so. Amen.

Stretch: Expand your consciousness my reflecting on the word **freedom**.

Day Twenty-Seven: Freedom

Thank heaven twenty seven! I don't know why I got the urge to say that, I just did. Sounds kind of catchy. Don't you think? Maybe it was because I'm still rhyming from yesterday, who knows? Anyway, this morning I got up and thanked the Lord that I was free. You see a lot of us are free, but we don't know that we're free. We're so busy focusing our energies on the things that hold us back. Hanging on to regrets, guilt, remorse and anger, and living in the past keeps us in bondage. It stops us from living in the present moment and distorts our outlook on the future. The idea of Freedom never gets a chance to register in the minds of some because it is almost impossible for them to grasp hold of something so magnificent.

Freedom, just like anything else, is a choice. Last night, I laid awake in bed for hours until finally I decided to get up and perhaps make use of my time by studying since I could not fall asleep. I pulled the string to open my vertical blinds. I saw two things. I saw the beautiful clear midnight blue sky. Tiny stars that sparkled were thrown all over it. I watched fluffy white clouds assume their position while airplanes breezed through them. Then I imagined myself on one of those airplanes, flying to a beautiful Island on a sunny breezy day so I could just rest there all day. It's amazing how people just get up and go in the middle of the night. They catch a plane to where ever for whatever reason. *That's Freedom.* The thought of me on that sunny island for a little R&R made me smile, because I realized that I am truly free; and so is everyone else. *Do you know what gives us freedom?* What gives us freedom is the wonderful gift of imagination.

A black Magnum passing by with extra boom in the base broke my concentration. It had the kind of base that rattles the windows to your house. As I shifted back into reality, I realized that I grew up with bars on the windows and doors of my house. According to my parents, our house had been robbed when I was just a toddler. Since then, bars were a necessity. Up until that point, I didn't realize just how much I did not like bars. My parents believed they were for our protection, but in moments like this, when I did notice them, I felt caged in. It was my imagination that often made the bars invisible.

Earlier that day, I went to visit a friend. The first thing I noticed was that he didn't have bars on his house. His house was triple the size of our house, and inside he had beautiful paintings worth hundreds and thousands of dollars. He had expensive cars parked in his garage, but he didn't have bars on the outsides of his house to protect him and his family. He walked me outside and I must have sounded like an idiot when I asked him, *"Why don't you have bars on your house?"* He questioned me back with the most puzzled look on his face. *"What do I need bars for?"* I felt like a peon when I realized that I had asked a man who was living his life from a state of consciousness that was free, why he didn't have bars on his house. *"I don't know. I was just asking."* You think with all of his expensive things that he would have an alarm system, pit bulls outside, fire weapons nearby, and yes… bars, at least the fancy decorative ones that we had on our house. Nope! He had no bars, no pit bulls, no alarm, or fire arms that I could see… and it was so refreshing.

It just goes to show that freedom really is a state of mind. To live in a state of freedom only means that you take the chains off of your mind. It means that you eliminate negative thinking. The thoughts that we think attract our experiences anyway. So why should he need bars if he doesn't rob folk, and think folks would rob him. I was really blown away when he told me that two of his neighbors had keys to his home, and he had keys to theirs. I admit I'm growing, but I cannot wait to grow to that level of mental freedom. Seeing that really inspired me, and it made me realize that if I want to truly be free, I need to ask God to help me trust Him enough to trust others. I'm just being real, I can't preach to you if I'm not willing to confront my own short comings.

I'll tell you about another free man I know. He was a good

friend of mine who was incarcerated for eleven years of his life. He also spent three of those years in solitary confinement. Do you know what happened to my friend while he was incarcerated? He learned to live from a consciousness of freedom. He lived freely in a cell, with a bunk bed, and a toilet in it. When his hands and feet were chained together in solitary confinement, he freed his mind and lived from there. The mind is so phenomenal. We can think ourselves into or out of anything. My friend traded stocks and made money when he was in prison. He obtained a barber's license and a personal trainer certificate while he was in prison. He finished high school in prison, and got his GED, and he also tutored and helped others do the same. He became a minister and helped restore the spirits of others while he was *locked down*. Freedom is wonderful, and we always have it. No one can take it away from us, unless we give it to them. My friend had accomplished more in the eleven years he was incarcerated than many of his friends who had never been inside of a prison.

On the flip side, I know a woman who's never even seen the inside of a prison, but when I tell you she's locked up, believe that the space she lives in is a very limited one. The fear, judgments, complaints, and the constant struggle, she puts herself through in order to be what she feels society depicts her to be, are prison walls that she can never seem to escape. It's as if a permanent rope is around her neck and it will not allow her to move without a fatal outcome. She resides in the worst prison with the worst conditions, those being the conditions of her mind. She seldom gets visitation because she is so critical, no one wants to be around her. She has sentenced herself to a life in prison, and she holds the key.

We can all chose freedom and truly live from that open space when we learn to control our thoughts. If we think ugly thoughts, we will take ourselves to the most dreadful places. We become criminals, because we are guilty for thinking illegally. It is illegal because God's law is universal. It is given freely to us. To think up and own erroneous thoughts and turn them into beliefs, is a crime that we commit all too often.   Those thoughts were not given to you freely by your Father God which means, to have acquired them, you had to break in and enter. That means that you went off sneaking into places where a child of God had no business. You stole something that was not yours. If you don't want to go to prison, and you want to remain free, don't take what does not belong to a child of God. If we do take what does not belong to us, we can only blame ourselves when we are sentenced.

***Exercise*:**   Close your eyes. Take a deep breath in through your nose and blow it out through your mouth. Just stand where you are. Feel your feet planted firmly on solid ground. As you focus your mind on your feet, move up to your ankles, your calves, your hamstrings, your quadriceps, your hips, your glutes, your lower back, and your abdomen. Stop there. Place both hands over your navel and inhale deeply. You should feel your stomach push out. Then blow out deeply through your mouth. You should feel your abdomen sink in. With your hands over abdomen, quietly say to yourself, "I release all tension from my body, because I am free." Now, as you focus your attention on that thought, slowly bring your hands back down to your sides. Focus your mind on your upper back, now your chest, your shoulders, your arms, and your hands. Wiggle your fingers and bring them up to your head. Spread your fingers apart, and place both hands over the top of your head. Now Affirm: My freedom is here. My freedom is here. My freedom is here because all of my thoughts are freeing. I release all that is debilitating, and limiting, and I accept everything that is good. I AM FREE. I am special because God has blessed me with freewill, so that I can live freely as long as I breathe. I accept my freedom. Freedom is the state of consciousness that I fully accept. Do this exercise until you truly feel free.

Cool Down: Deny with me: Nothing outside of me can hurt me. Nothing outside of me has power over me. Nothing can control me, and nothing is holding me back. Everything that I need to live a full and prosperous life is inside of me. I am free because God said so. I am the only one who can put myself in prison. I chose to be free. I chose to be free. I AM FREE. FREEDOM IS MY BIRTH RIGHT. And so it is!

Stretch: Expand your consciousness by concentrating on the idea of **love**.

Day Twenty-Eight: Love

I love you. That's easy for me to say because I understand what love is. It's also easy for me to say because I love myself. I love my strengths, and the parts of me that I need to spend extra time with. When we understand what love is and how loving ourselves helps us to love and appreciate others, then the idea of love won't be so difficult to understand. Remember what love is. To say the least, love is patient and kind. The preacher at my church described Love as the idea of oneness. With this I agree. This is why it is so important for us to love ourselves first. When we love ourselves, we gather our broken parts together and allow them to heal.

As we make our selves whole, we better understand the reason and roles that others play in our lives. You may not realize this but love can also be associated with work. It can be associated with work because it is a process. In most cases, it is unlikely for love to happen overnight. Love requires action. Take a relationship for example. A couple vows to spend the rest of their lives together. That is a heck of a commitment. Do you honestly believe that every day they wake up, they are going to want to hug and kiss? Surely not. However, the action of hugging and kissing helps the *idea* of love to sink in. His gesture of open arms sets the tone for acceptance, and kindness, and oneness to take place again. The idea of making love is often a conscious act of coming together.

Nothing can live without Love. Did you know that if you don't hug or caress an infant, it will die? The same concept is true for a pet. If you don't interact, and pet your family pet, it will die. A couple of days ago, I went to a park nearby to jog. The amount of love that I saw at that place really overwhelmed me. It was absolutely breath *giving*. When I go there, I normally do five or six laps around the trail, but as I became besieged by all of the love that surrounded me, it gave me energy to continue to press along. I must have done fifteen laps easily.

To be honest, I lost count. I just know that I got out there at about 6:30, and I left after dark.

Smiling to myself, I remember when the people who lived in the neighborhood were primarily of Hispanic decent. I loved the park so much because of the vastness of all the natural beauty it possessed. I used to just go and sit, and watch my Cuban and Dominican brothers play soccer. They were there playing soccer that night as well. However, they had some Haitian brothers on the team, with a sprinkle of Caucasian brothers as well. All though the game is always entertaining, tonight it was simply splendid. I enjoyed watching that game. It was like watching a rainbow run all over the sky, ducking and dodging little rain drops. Then I looked over by the swing set. There was an African American family having a birthday party for a toddler. The little Hispanic kids kept running over asking for birthday cake, and the lady kept feeding them until their mothers interjected. It was awesome! As I began to stretch, a group of guys passed me by. The one that was leading the pack winked his blue eyes at me. I winked back. That was fun I thought, as I got in my car and rolled out of the parking lot, and you know what else? That was all love.

Exercise: Today make a conscious effort to be a part of the love movement. Let's help Dr. Martin Luther King's dream stay alive. Today make a conscious effort to restrain from subtle prejudice and discrimination. The sooner we erase all error from our minds, the faster the love will flow. While creating a love consciousness, these are some things to remember. In order to stop criticizing others, you must stop criticizing yourself. Remember it is possible to accept yourself while making changes. Hating yourself while trying to change will only stagnate your efforts. Try hard to see the good in all people, even those that get under your skin. Most importantly, remember that God loves us despite our imperfections so we should do the same for our brothers and sisters.

Cool Down: Affirm: I love and accept myself exactly as I am. I am worthy of love. I freely give love, and accept love just as readily as I give it. (After repeating this five times, write this truth statement in bold letters, and post it somewhere that it will be visible to you for the next fourteen days.)

Stretch: Expand your consciousness by reflecting on the word ***beauty***.

Day Twenty-Nine: Beauty

In case you haven't heard it in a while, I'm telling you that you are beautiful. According to your standards of beauty, I'm sure you all look better than you did when you first started this journey. More importantly I know that if you feel like me, you feel renewed as well. YOU ARE BEAUTIFUL. Remember that!

I remember coming up as a little girl. My classmates and the neighborhood children would have me think I was the ugliest thing alive. Children can be so mean. I guess it's what they are taught at home. Or maybe it's a defense mechanism; before someone gets the opportunity to say something bad about them, they say something hurtful out of fear. For the parents out there, be sure you teach your children not to call their peers names, and protect your children from those children whose parents don't teach them not to call names by calling your children wonderful names, like genius, superstar, handsome, king, and queen etc.

As a child, I caught the school bus home. I never forget there was a bully on our bus who had it in for me big time. For what? I haven't a clue. I never did a thing to the poor child. She called me blacky, buttery teeth, skinny, lizard lips, booty lips, and bald headed. Her words stuck with me all throughout elementary school. One day she must have really had a bad day, because that day she was extra mean. She waited until I got on the second step to get on the bus, and she looked me dead in my eyes and said, "You are so ugly it's a shame. If I ever have a baby and it looks like you, I'll throw it in the garbage." Then she pushed me down the steps, and I fell on my back in front of everybody.

I don't have children. I admit that being a parent has to be one of the toughest jobs next to being a spouse. All the decisions you have to make, have to be hard. I often wonder how I would discipline my children if and when I have some. I always say I don't want to spank my kids, but if my child did something like that to another child.... God give me the strength is all that I can say. I remember I brought some of that crap home to my house, and the first time I called one of my sisters a *black something* my mother was all over my head with a shoe in the back seat of the car. I can't say that it helped much, because everything I had been called in school, I probably came home and repeated it to one of my younger siblings when they got on my nerves. I called my younger siblings names because I hated what I saw in the mirror. I remember I would have this re-occurring dream that my skin had become two shades lighter and my hair had grown in two long ponytails. Every time I had that dream I'd jump out of bed, and look in the mirror only to find that I was still too black, and all of my hair did not fit into a ponytail. Of course, this made me sad and angry, so I took it out on those around me.

As I got older, I wondered who teaches us what beauty is. Do we learn it? Do we get it from the television? What message are we sending to our children about what is beautiful? I suffered a great deal coming up. By the time I had reached middle school, I knew I was the ugliest girl there. People had no problem affirming my belief. By this time, I was ugly and angry. Now I was fighting to be beautiful. Any and every body that called me blacky, bald headed, buck teeth, or whatever was going to get my fist in their mouths. I spent a lot of time in detention in middle school. I always got my work done, but I did it in CSI, or detention.

By eight grade, I had started to grow breast, and my booty was starting to get a little fatter. The boys didn't seem to mind now that I didn't have long hair or had an over bite, covered by big booty lips. The only thing they cared about was that it was mango season. In high school, my looks were still the same but for some reason or another, high school boys appreciated big lips and didn't seem to have a complexion preference. I guess it would be obvious that I loved high school, and I did exceptionally well there. I stayed out of trouble and I did my work. I also excelled in every extracurricular activity they had.

Yet and still, my self-worth was dependant on how many boys thought I was beautiful. My beauty was still in *their* hands. Luckily, all the boys in my high school wanted the same thing. They wanted a girl with a big butt and big breast, and a nice smile, and that's exactly what I had. I managed to graduate from high school with only a cut or two.

Now in my early 20s, things changed. All of my friends were still guys because they seemed to find beauty in everything and everybody. I liked the way they thought. We could be sitting down having lunch and a woman would pass by and my guy friend would say she was beautiful. Another woman would pass by and he'd say the same, and another and another and another. I looked at these women and I could not understand why my guy friends thought all of them were beautiful. To my *learned* critical eye, the first one had too much fat around her stomach. The next one could use some braces, to close the gap in her teeth. The one after that looked like her face would be better suited without those *hard looking dreads*, and the one after that was straight up *ugly*. My guy friend told me that I did not understand beauty. He said that variety makes things beautiful. He told me I actually looked a whole lot better *before* I bleached my skin, and lost twenty pounds. He also said that braids looked better on me, but admitted that my face was pretty enough to have any style suit it. When I had braces he would always tell me to smile. His favorite picture of me is a picture I had when I had just started twisting my natural hair, and when I wore braces. It was the first time that I saw snow. I was so elated that when he snapped the picture I wasn't even paying attention. When I asked him why he liked that picture out of all of the other ones that I had taken, he said it was because in that picture I wasn't *trying* to be beautiful. He said that day I actually felt beautiful, and that's when my beauty showed the most.

To think as women we go through so many changes trying to look like someone else. Because we were taught what was beautiful, we try and emulate that. I can't tell you how many times I have changed myself based on someone else's opinion. It's terrible. Now whether or not my friend thinks my hair looks better braided or he thinks I look better wearing braces, is really none of my concern. We should not be concerned with making changes based on what *others* think or say. We definitely should not change our appearances to try and emulate someone else's. It ruins our authenticity.

I've arrived to this conclusion. If I feel like perming my hair, I'll perm my hair. If I feel like growing my perm out and twisting my natural hair, I'll do that. If I want to get a weave job done down to my ankles, I'll do that. It's my business. The same goes for my body. For the last couple of weeks, all I've been wanting to do is run and stretch. Nothing else. Of course that's going to shape my body differently than if I was weight training three to four times a week, but it's all good. *I accept me now*. All of me. The changes that I make now are because I want to try something different, or because my mood is this way or that. It has nothing to do with the woman next to me, or the man in front of me. These changes that we go through, because we feel we need to be someone else, is tearing us apart and has us totally focused on the wrong things in life. We spend too much time trying to copy the beauty in the movies and magazines rather than polishing and flaunting our own natural beauty, which can create a new image to put on the cover of a magazine. In your next attempt to change your appearance, remember that beauty is not a look. Beauty is a feeling of self-worth that begins in the mind and exudes to the surface, giving you that glow that no exfoliate can give.

I have to tell this story as it is one that I always wanted to tell, and it relates to the subject. I remember when I was dating my ex-fiancé. He had a friend who I thought was the epitome of beauty. At 21, I was still making my own changes to the outer part of myself. I guess you can say that I was doing a whole lot of working out with almost no exercise. I already told you I was bleaching my skin, whitening my teeth, buying the most expensive weaves, and losing a lot of weight. Basically, I was trying to fix what the bully had told me I needed to fix. Anyway, this woman was beautiful in my eyes. She was everything I was not. She was mixed. I don't know what she was mixed with. I just know her hair was long, she had fair skin, and straight white teeth. She had a super tight tummy which made her implants look very large. Not only that, she was really a nice person. The thing is I was very insecure with myself. It appeared to me that she was trying to take *my* man. They were just friends; but I had forbid him to be her friend. I made up all kind of delusional stories as to why they could not be friends. I told him she looked at me this way, or she said this when he wasn't looking. The two were friends before he and I even met. If something would have been there between them, then you would've thought it would have already happened. It hadn't. I was so afraid, however, that it would, because she was so beautiful, and I believed I was so ugly. My heart dropped to my stomach every time this woman came around my fiancé. The sight of her drove me up the wall. One day I told my fiancé the truth. I just told him about my history and how I felt about myself, and how *she* made me feel. The man was baffled. "Are you kidding me?" he wanted to know. When tears came to my eyes, he knew I wasn't making up stories. He assured me and all that, but you know when you don't have your own self assurance, no one else's assurance is good enough. He even agreed to stop all the small talk that was going on between the two of them. I realized this was a problem that I needed to fix. Every day when I saw her, I forced myself to say hello, no matter how badly I wanted to punch her in the face. She was always polite and humbly bowed her head and spoke back. This went on for months. No real conversations just the cordial speaking, *which I admit for me was still enough.* I wasn't going to go inviting her to our house or anything. I'm a child of God, not stupid. God blessed us all with discernment, and I ain't afraid to use it!

One day I was working out and she walked up to me and then she asked me, "How do you get your butt to sit up like that?" I'm thinking to myself, I sure didn't do what you did to get your breast to sit up like that. I couldn't say it because that would have been very immature. Even if I was immature, there was no reason for me to act immature. So

I told her the truth. A lot of it was genetics, and I also do a lot of squats and lunges. When she told me that she had always been jealous of my butt, I told her that I really admired how pretty she always kept her hair. When she asked if she and I could work out together sometimes, I agreed, but neither of us ever made any plans. We'd pass each other in the gym, and I'd catch her watching me do my squats, and she'd catch me watching her tie up her hair. Beauty is in the eye of the beholder, and she was beautiful, but so was I.

Exercise: Affirm with me 100 times! I AM Beautiful just the way God created me. Repeat it 100 times. You've got all day. For more power, you should say this while you look yourself in the eye in the mirror butt naked.

Cool Down: Affirm: Beauty is in the eye of the beholder and I behold my own beauty first.

Stretch: Expand your consciousness by meditating on the word *now*.

Day Thirty: Now

For the last thirty days, I've woke up every morning looking forward to speaking to you. Because I so readily anticipated our meeting, some days I would become a little anxious. While subtle anxiety is natural and will keep you on your toes, antagonizing anxiety can bring you to a complete *involuntary* halt.

I've learned that when I feel myself getting too anxious, it is time for me to stop everything! I stop everything and I just breathe. As I become calm, I ask myself what needs to be done at this point. I find that I only get incredibly anxious when I start thinking about everything that I must do today, next week, next month, and next year. At that point I'm not cognizant that the things that I'm thinking about can and will be spread out in the future, no matter what I do now. It is because I'm thinking about them so intensely, my brain is feeding me the signal that they need to be done *NOW*. At this point my perception is that everything is so urgent, that if I don't take action now, at this very second, my world is going to cave in. What kind of faith is that; and where is this all powerful God that I can call on for help when things get heavy? That just goes to show you that even the best of us tend to forget sometimes.

My goal is for us to remember that the most important time we have is now. The present moment is the only moment that has true power. Yes, we may let ourselves be affected by the past, and in most cases, past experiences do shape our attitudes and behaviors when it deals with our relationship to the future. If you're anything like me, we often think about the future, and what's to come. Personally, I don't like to dwell too much in the past, but I am guilty when it comes to getting a little ahead of myself. However, I find that the present is often overlooked because our heads are turn behind us, or we're standing on our tippy-toes trying to see far ahead of us. Now, becomes unimportant, and overlooked. When we look in the past or focus solely on the future, we miss the gifts of the present moment. Indulgence, in the present moment, is the key to bringing forth the best future we can possibly imagine.

I agree that having something to look forward to heightens our expectations for tomorrow--giving us direction, and aspiration for the future. However, the present moment is the stepping stone for a solid foundation for the future. Think about it, what happened yesterday cannot be undone, and tomorrow is yet to come. The only way the past can serve us is from the lessons we learn from them.

My mom and dad used to say to us coming up, *"We plan a plan and Allah plans a plan, and surely Allah is the best of planners."* All they were saying was be open to spirit and don't be attached to an outcome. That, I understood well. This is why I still made goals for myself and, yes, I gave myself a time to achieve them but I didn't become inundated with the procedure itself. For a better quality of life, it is important to make every second of our lives count, and we can only do that moment by moment. To live this way is the only peaceful, loving, and harmonious approach to life.

I'll never forget the day I decided to take a long leave of absence from my job. Everyday I'd wake up when my body got ready. I didn't set an alarm clock or anything. I just let my body wake me up. After almost two years of waking up at 4:00 am by alarm, this time was much deserved. When I woke up, I just sat in bed and told God how much I love Him, and how much I thank Him for everything. I wouldn't rush His response. I just waited for Him to guide and direct me. Once I got my direction, I simply grabbed my journal and wrote down what it was that He had told me today. Then I went to the kitchen, drank ten ounces of water, and grabbed an apple. By the time I got back to my room and finished my apple, I had thought up more than one way to accomplish the task. You want to know something else? Sometimes, the task got done that day, and sometimes it did not. As seconds turned into minutes, and minutes turned into hours, more was revealed. I continued to receive direction from Him, and I still got His work done. I woke up the same way, day in and day out. It's funny how the Lord works. If I didn't complete the thing that he told me to get done on that particular day, He would tell me to do it again on this day. This day, it was easier to get it done. All the resources were in place. All the angels were out. Sometimes, God just wants to put something in our hearts and on our minds until NOW arrives. This is why it is very important to listen and obey. God knows when you are trying. He also knows when you are being a tad bit lackadaisical.

The very project that I'm working on right now was revealed to me four or five years ago. Had I embarked on it then, which I had every intention to do, it would have just been another quick fix diet and nutrition plan for you. It would have been missing some very valuable stories. It was only because I waited that you could have a piece of my soul to go along with your forty-day get in shape plan. I'm glad I was patient. I'm glad that I gave myself time to grow, and I'm glad I did not regret that I didn't complete it when it was revealed to me.

Now, from what I just told you, it may sound like a contradiction but I want you to know that I believe in ambition, progress, and seizing the moment; but I know you have to be very quiet and listen to that still small voice that does not like to scream. That voice, that inner knowing, will never fail you. She'll never have you rush out on a whim, because for her she's too confident to act on urgency. She'll always guide you now because she can see the future that you can't see, even if you stood on your tippy toes.

I had a friend that would become agitated with me because I didn't move fast enough for him. He was into progress, expansion, and fast decision making. My friend was obsessed with the future. He worked very hard to *secure* it. When it was all said and done, he agreed that some of what he did was okay, but if he could do it again he would have waited. I just smiled and told him not to regret, because regretting is living in the past. He couldn't get the things that he lost back. He could, however, learn from his mistakes today.

On the other hand, I know a woman who, until this day, lives in the past. She is so smart, beautiful, and talented. None of that matters though because she can't see it. She only sees the past. She only sees what happened to her, what someone has done to her, or what she believes people owe her. She only sees why she can't get ahead. Every day, she tries to get yesterday back and, every day, she is unsuccessful. If you tell her to let go, she will become upset. If you try to teach her something fresh and new, she can't seem to grasp the concept. Her life is at a point that I call stagnation.

The past is gone. The future is not here, but **now** is waving its little arms in front of you saying, *"Hey you, I'm right here. Do something with me. Don't worry. I'll lead you into the future."* Don't be like the woman living in the past. Pay attention to what's in front of you because **now** is the gift that matters. **Now** will always be around, that is if you don't get stuck in the past, or exhaust yourself rushing for the future.

Exercise: Pray with me: God, thank you for this moment. I release the past and I use now wisely, knowing that you are directing my path for a glorious future. I accept this as so. And so it is.

Cool Down: Pray with me: Thank you God for this moment. Amen

Stretch: Expand your consciousness by reflecting on the idea of *forgiveness*.

FALL

FALL

The Law of Forgiveness

We're here. The last ten days of our journey have arrived. Like a long run to the destination of choice, it always seems as if getting started is the hardest part. However, when you're on your way back home, the run feels so easy. It's like your legs aren't even moving. It's all mental. Your mind *knows* to run and your body just obeys. These last ten days will be a breeze so you don't have to fret. Just remain beautiful, relaxed, and let's enjoy our last days together on this journey.

The exercises for these last ten days will be simple but very effective. For the last ten days, we won't need a Warm Up or a Cool Down. The real work has been done. In these last ten days, the exercises are for relaxation and defining. Most of you won't even break a sweat. Although Warm Ups and Cool Downs will be discarded in this season, stretching will still be included. I find it to be true in fitness, as well as in life, that while we may not always have the time to Warm Up and Cool Down, it is inevitable that exercise and stretching will always be a requirement for progress and growth.

Forgiveness is a spiritual law that we must put into practice every day of our lives. No matter how bad things seem, or how badly we believe that we have been wronged, letting go is crucial for our emotional well being. If you want to live a life that is spiritually based, then forgiveness is a requirement.

The woman who could have been my mother in law gave me and my ex- fiancé some good advice. She said never go to bed angry with each other. She said before you close your eyes and turn your back to each other, talk to each other. If you all don't feel like talking, at least pray for each other and then go to sleep. At twenty two, I really didn't understand what she was saying. Five years later, her words opened up in front of me like a rose in spring time. All she was saying was *forgive*.

She was saying release negative toxins from your body by freeing your mind. She was saying don't hold a grudge. Don't hold on to a memory or thought that can only produce feelings that make your body sick.

Many of us think that to forgive is to be weak. We believe that if we forgive someone, we are letting them use us as a doormat. This is not the case with forgiveness. When you learn the art of forgiveness, it acts as a unifier in your life. It helps you to see the good in all people, including yourself. I don't know if you can relate, but in my own experience, when I had a hard time forgiving others, I had a hard time forgiving myself. I also had a difficult time loving and accepting myself. I was very critical of myself. I projected the same feelings of dislike on almost everyone that I met. Understand that just because I practice forgiveness, it does not excuse me from getting upset from time to time. It's just a little different now. Now it's easier for me to detach the person from their action. The same concept applies when I deal with myself. If my emotions get the best of me and I say something to someone that I wouldn't have ordinarily said, yes for a minute there may be feelings of remorse; but then forgiveness allows me to see that *I* am not *what* I did or said yesterday. What I did yesterday was a reaction to what I was feeling. *I, however, am not my actions or my feelings,* so I can start again. Every second of every day, if need be, I can start all over and show the world who I really am, and so can you.

If *anything* in your life is going to work, especially *relationships,* forgiveness is key. There is no way around it. People are going to be people; and it is important to understand that people are going to go through changes. The process of change is not always a comfortable one. It hurts sometimes. As a matter of fact, often times, it is very uncomfortable. This is why I incorporate stretching whenever we meet, because stretching makes you stronger and more pliable at the same time, making injuries less likely. The more you expand, the less rigid you are when it comes to dealing with change.

Forgiving someone is like saying, "Sweetheart, this situation that happened between us is not bigger than the good that God has in store for both of our lives." Forgiveness is our free insurance to a greater quality of life, because when we forgive, we are limiting our chances of harboring guilt, shame, anger, anxiety, rage, and hostility, which are all fear. Fear can create some nasty dysfunctions in the body. When you forgive, you are letting go of a heavy load and surrendering to God. When you forgive, you are being courageous and activating faith in God, therefore, disarming any power in the current circumstance.

Forgiveness is not the easiest thing to do, especially if you or someone close to you was hurt very badly. Even still, for your own sake, you *need* to forgive, no matter how heinous the act. For heaven sake, Jesus was nailed to a cross, and He looked down on the ignorant ones and asked God to forgive them, because they didn't understand what they were doing, and it's just that. We look at people and give them so much credit, assuming that they know what they're doing because they're an adult, a professional, and have a lot of letters behind their name, but that's hardly ever the case. People act according to their limited knowledge. People who are hurt and ignorant don't understand their foolish behavior.

I once heard of a pediatrician who molested his patients. When the parents found out, of course, they wanted to kill him. While gathering evidence for trial, it was later found that the doctor had been molested for most of his childhood. I'm not excusing his actions. I'm just saying that most of the time when people act, they act from a subconscious level. Normally, they treat people how they were treated or the way they feel.

Releasing people's foolish behavior from your mind is extremely important because when you hold on to it, you replay it again and again and again. In actuality, it only happened once. By holding the thought in mind after it has already died you are *resurrecting* it. Remember "thoughts held in mind produce after its kind." The longer you hold that thought in mind, it will produce events and people in your life that you will need to forgive for similar reasons. Like attracts like. That is the Law. Resurrection is not limited to the physical; it is also a mental process. Take a moment and give some thought to the thoughts in your life that were dead and gone, that suddenly came up again in your life.

Most of the things that can change our lives for the better involve a process. They take time to learn and grow into. This is true for forgiveness. The sooner we get started, the sooner we will live the lives that God intended for us to live. The process starts with you. I know you're probably saying I'm not the one who did wrong, it was so and so. That may be true; but consider this. It is important to forgive yourself first. Forgiving yourself first detaches you from the outcome. You see once you have forgiven yourself the way the other person reacts holds no merit. The reason you forgive yourself first is because everyone's heart is not soft. Some people behave grudge fully, because they haven't made forgiveness a practice in their own personal lives. Resentment has made them revengeful. People riddled with this poisonous mindset will hold you in contempt just to make you feel as miserable as they are. This is why it is important to honor yourself first, by forgiving yourself first. This practice directs your attention inward, thereby making it easier for you to forgive another. To forgive yourself means that you deal with the thoughts and feelings that caused you to act or respond distastefully to begin with. You forgive yourself for thinking the thought and believing the lies that brought about the negative experience in your life.

Here's an example. One of my friends married a man who reminded her of her father. My friend never got along with her father, and she carried a lot of resentment for him deep in her heart. She married a man who presented and revealed every insecurity that she had about herself, many of which, her father had pointed out to her. As a child, she felt as if she could not talk to her father. As an adult, she felt as if she could not talk to her husband. As a child, her father spent most of his time out of town. As an adult, her husband worked away from home for months at a time as well. In her own mind, she became very resentful of her spouse because she had gotten the two of them mixed up. In her frustration, she often cursed her husband, and sometimes she would even hit him. By the time she realized what she was doing, the two of them had separated. In her attempt to heal herself, she needed to forgive herself first, not for her actions, but for the thoughts and feelings that caused her to act in such a manner. Once she forgave herself for her actions, she was able to ask forgiveness of her husband. Although they did get back together to work on their marriage, her husband often brought up her short comings, those that she had asked his forgiveness for already. It was only because she had forgiven herself that she was able to find inner strength. She requested more time away from the marriage to continue to heal. If she would not have forgiven herself, his words would have done more damage than had already been done. It takes tremendous effort and mental endurance to forgive yourself. The world would always have you look at the things you've done wrong as opposed to those things that you've done right. I've never been incarcerated but I had a friend who was. When he told me that even after he served his time in prison, and did his time on probation, he still could not vote, I just thought to myself it just goes to show that it is important to forgive yourself every single chance you get; because, if you don't, you're exposed to the unforgiving hearts of others.

God's will for us is good, all the time no matter the circumstance. Remember this, because forgiveness is tricky. You'll try to forgive yourself and someone will throw something in your face that will make you feel guilty. You'll try to forgive someone and they'll do something else that will make you upset again. In this case don't waste too much energy trying to fix it. Instead, go to God. Ask Him to honor your intentions to make amends and move on in confidence, assured that He is taking care of everyone involved. And always remember, forgiveness does not mean reconciliation. It would be nice, but it's not always the case.

Forgiveness needs to be practiced everywhere--in our homes, neighborhoods, in traffic, and even on our jobs. So many people hate their jobs simply because of the stressful work environment which is caused by the many misunderstandings that happen in the work place. I had two situations at work in which I had to practice forgiveness in order to make my stay at work more peaceful.

There was a new employee that came in who needed to build her referral base. I offered to help her by giving her an account that I had been working a couple months prior. My schedule changed so I could no longer do the outreach program on the weekend. She was available so it was an excellent trade-off. I still wanted to close the account on a corporate level, but if you've ever tried to close a corporate account, you know that they are truly a work in progress. *I understood* that I was giving her the outreach on the weekends. I figured that would help her gain some clientele. However, *she understood* that I was giving her the entire account. I realized this when her demeanor changed after I had submitted the account information to the corporate analyst. So I did what I do best. I attempted to talk to her. When she was alone, of course, in the break room I accompanied her there and brought to her attention what I thought was bothering her. I was correct but she insisted that I not worry about it. I took her advice until things began to get out of hand. Gossip led to negative attention that I did not want. I turned over the whole account to her and went on being successful in my work. This seemed to aggravate the situation even more. So I tried again, talking that is, but this time my efforts were met with a little more hostility and resistance. So I backed away. When people don't want to talk, it's not our job to make them talk. At this point, we should simply walk away and seek God's help.

One of the things I love about the application of forgiveness is the fact that we "for-give." We give up control for a higher reward. We cease to control the situation when we give it to God. Looking back on the situation with my co-worker I realized that I tried to control the way she perceived me. This is what led me to give her my account in the first place. Then I tried to control her by urging her to talk to me so that I could further control the amount of gossip that had started in the office as a result of our misunderstanding.

Whenever we believe that we need to forgive someone else, there is always an opportunity for us to forgive ourselves. When it got right down to it, I felt guilty about being the highest producer while she and some of the other employees seemed to struggle. While I liked being number one, it was lonely and I wanted her and my other co-workers to like me. In essence, my attempt to give her my leads and my corporate account was my sorry attempt to people please. I had to forgive myself for that. Her attitude towards me was just a projection of the way I felt about my own success.

When I went home I cried, but then I prayed. I admitted my mistakes and then I got up, found my mirror and looked myself in the eyes and said, "I'm sorry for abusing you like that. I love you and I will not let it happen again. Now I want you to go back to work and continue to be the success that you are and never give anything away that was given to you, because you want someone to like you." I admit I cried a little bit more, and then I fell asleep. The next day, I went to work. I spoke the way I did every morning. I did not feel the need to make individual trips to anyone's desk. That morning, I was free. I had forgiven myself, and I had nothing else to say to anyone. I open my daily inspiration and coincidently, it spoke on forgiveness. It read:

"Let Bygones be Bygones. When conflict or disagreement comes up, it is easy to believe the other person is wrong. Jesus told us to stop looking at the speck in another's eye and deal with ourselves. Whatever the situation, I play a role: What is my part here? What baggage did I bring? What preconceived notion is preventing me from adopting another way of thinking?

If I am going to lay down my sword and shield and stop studying war, I must be willing to let bygones be bygones. Whoever hurt me, however I failed to meet any expectations, it is done. What can I do NOW? Even if I am alone in seeking and applying a resolution, it is still important for me to undertake one.

No matter the attitude of anyone else, I can be secure in knowing that revenge is not my concern. The laws of God will bring divine justice (which I may or may not understand). My faith and God's love for me allows me to accept all with joy.

For He will repay according to each ones deeds: to those who by patiently doing good seek for glory, and honor, and immortality, He will give eternal life." Romans 2:6-7

I had to read that about three times and let it sink in. Once it did, Spirit said write a letter to her, attach the daily word and leave it. That's just what I did. The letter read:

Dear Ms. So and So,

I don't know what really happened between us, but something did. As you can imagine, I don't like conflict. My intent was to help, but maybe I did more harm than good. I read this this morning, and I thought it applied, so I am giving it to you. I'm not saying that we need to hang out or go to lunch together. What I am saying, however, is we don't need the unnecessary conflict. Let's let bygones be bygones. I forgive you and I bless you and I release you to your greatest good.

Sincerely,

Nadirah

Words were not exchanged between us that day or any other day except for the good morning that we'd give to everyone in the office. Other than that, we did our jobs. I don't know about her, but I was relieved and happy. I knew where I messed up, and I had done my ground work. All I know is weeks later, she quit. She never said goodbye or responded to the letter, but I still called it all to the good.

On a more positive note, some of the best friendships are built on the foundation of forgiveness. I had the great pleasure of working with a woman name Kathy. Kathy was an older woman, and I admit she taught me everything about the system by which our company was run. When I first started working there, I was enrolling people left and right, and I was stepping on a lot of toes as well, because I didn't understand the system. The rule was the person had to have an appointment with the counselor in order for the counselor to sign them up. I knew people from everywhere so when I saw a friend, I waved them down, and they came and enrolled with me. The problem was those were other people's appointments. I really had no idea. Almost everyone in the office was upset with me because, according to the system, I was stealing their guest. One day, Kathy got really upset, and she told me a thing or two. Instantly, I became upset with her, but I refrained from telling her a thing or two, myself. Instead, I explained to her that I had no idea about the system and how it was run. I thought my job was just to sell. That had always been the protocol of my previous employers. So, she went over everything with me, and I recognized where I had gone wrong. I asked her for her help. She happily obliged. When traffic was slow, Kathy would go over company protocol with me. I would give Kathy sales tips. If I forgot to bring cash to work, Kathy would buy me lunch, and vice versa. We even got to the point of referring clients to one another on our days off. That was a huge stress relief for the both of us. Knowing that we can make money on our days off, and trust someone to take care of your client was the best. All this happened because we chose to let bygones be bygones and move on. It was a blessing to be able to move on the way we did. It made our job a whole lot easier. I have so many forgiveness stories I could go on and on, but for now I'll stop here. I just want to say this-- become a radical forgiver.

Don't even think about it. I bet you your quality of life will increase for the good.

Denial for the Fall

"*There is nothing in the universe for me to fear, for greater is He that is within me than he that is in the world.*" I love this. This statement is a denial, but it also affirms our strength and courage. No matter how puny your muscle may appear to be, understand that within you greatness resides. Your heart beats greatness. You inhale and exhale greatness. Greatness runs through your veins. The good ideas that you conjure up in your mind and have courage to see through *are* your greatness. Those ideas will bring you into your God-Self. That who you really are. It is the "I AM" of your being. Maybe you have not tapped into it yet. It could be that you are tapping into it right now. Some of you are fortunate to have been living from that place since childhood.

No matter where you are or what you encounter, God is everywhere evenly present. So that means He is in you. Be confident in this truth so that you may stand up to the world and say "I AM that I AM because ALL MIGHTY GOD said so. He is my father and I am like Him". *Only when you realize this, wallow around in this, jump up and down in this, and sit down quietly and concentrate on this, will you be able to make your demonstration*! When you are doing the will of God, the world cannot and will not want to stop you. In fact, they will beckon for your help, and support you in your work. When you do work that you love, and work that is uplifting to mankind, the universe begins to dance to your beat. The q*uestion is will you be afraid to create music.* I hope not because there is so much more for us to do than we can even begin to think of. This life needs you! So have NO FEAR!

Affirmation for the Fall

"God works in me to will and do whatever He wishes to do, and He cannot fail." Anything that is positive, beautiful, and that will breathe hope in the hearts of man, that is in your heart to do, don't delay! Get busy. If you only knew. That is not your desire, that is God speaking through you to get His work done. You should feel honored that He has handpicked you for this important mission. He chose you because He believes you are strong enough! He knows you are capable! He has outfitted you personally for the position! It is only you who believes that you are unemployed. When you work for God, you always have a job that pays well, and has awesome benefits!

We silence the desires of our hearts and we put our dreams on the back burner, because we still look at ourselves as *inconspicuous, small, uneducated, unimportant and incapable.* The sooner we accept that we are here to serve God, the more seriously we will value ourselves and our work. I told you I was born into a Muslim home. When I asked my mother and father what the word Muslim means, and they told me that a Muslim was one who sacrificed his personal will to serve Allah/ God, I thought about it. At fifteen years old, you don't necessarily want to give up all of your pleasures for the pleasures of this *God* you can't see. As I got older and understood the significance of sacrifice, and understood that God was not a condemning God, I made peace with calling myself a Muslim. If that is the true definition of Muslim, then I can say that I know Christians who are Muslim. I know Jews who are Muslim. I know people who don't identify with any religion at all who are better Muslims than the Muslims that I was raised around.

My name often raises many questions about my ethnicity. When I tell people it is a *muslim* name, the first thing they ask me is am I a Muslim. I simply respond, *almost* because I am a student with many lessons to learn. I can count on one hand the true Muslims that I've met in my life, and it's ironic that half of them don't identify with any religious discipline at all.

I ask you again. WHO IS YOUR FATHER? WHO DO YOU RECEIVE YOUR INSTRUCTIONS FROM, and WHO ARE YOU HERE TO SERVE? Many of us are still serving the ego, which is why we can't honestly call ourselves, a Muslim, a Christian, a Buddhist, or anything else that requires us to give up the physical self and live for the Lord. We say we were trying to serve God, but this is an untruth. We tell ourselves this because we think we can trick God. I did that and, sometimes, I still do without even realizing it. *Nadirah* lived for her ego and that would have been her fate. God, however, stepped in and sent Aqueelah to help Nadirah. Only then was she able to see that the work she claimed she was doing for God was vanity work she was doing to nurse the ego. When God, the true intelligence factor, stepped in, Nadirah-Aqueelah was able to live life as God intended.

If it were left up to me, I'd be working my 9-5 Monday-Friday and on the weekends, I'd be in somebody's theatre, or perhaps, I'd be laid out on the beach--but no. Now is not the time for that. I have work to do, and might I tell you, I love what I do! I remember asking God to use me to do *His* work. I asked God to show me how I can connect with and empower my brothers and sisters. While in this book, I speak to my sisters, God has revealed many ways for me to connect with my brothers, and I am ready and so excited. People think that you have to be a scholar to speak the word of God. This is a stifling belief that keeps the understanding and wisdom of those without a college education in silence. I refuse. Every experience you encounter and *grow* through is a lesson learned that you can teach. Every book that you have read and understood is the wisdom of God given to you so that you may shed light. Every gift and natural talent that you were born with is a gift from God. God has given you those gifts and talents to ensure that you are able to provide for yourself and your family. I thank God for institutions like universities and schools to further my knowledge, or shall I say receive a certificate to make my knowledge credible, because even if I'm not enrolled in a system, I still study and then practice to show myself improved. But before there were colleges and universities, mankind did well trading gifts and talents. We get so caught up on being civilized, God forbid we have to go back to bartering and trading just so we can get the point. GOD WORKS IN

US TO DO HIS WILL AND WHAT EVER HE WISHES TO DO AND HE CANNOT FAIL! Are you going to turn that power over to the authorities? Who is your authority anyway? I say this with humility and no disrespect to local authorities, but God is my authority!

God is your authority, and He cannot fail. God gives us insight, and Spirit directs our path making it easy for us to get the *seemingly impossible* done. I could never fail, because I am made in the image and likeness of God, and God uses me in my physical form (body) continually to do His will on earth. That's why I say, 'get your body right'. The body is not some decorative object that we use to hang the latest fashions and platinum chains from. The body is the vehicle that shelters our hearts, and from our hearts spills forth the issues of life. The body transports and protects the mind where our thoughts reside. The totality of all of this is the soul. Wouldn't you want your precious soul to be transported in the most radiant, and energetic body. Surely you would, or you would not have picked up this book.

We cannot fail and God makes this evident by the way He designed our bodies. Our body is self renewing. In fact, within a couple of years, every cell in our body is completely renewed, giving us a new body. We are the ones who destroy it, with poisonous things like drugs, alcohol, cigarettes, processed foods, white sugar, high sodium, and large consumption of red meat. We do the same things to our minds. We hold on to negative thoughts, and turn them into negative beliefs about ourselves. We refuse to explore another way of thinking until the mental discord becomes so painful that it forces us to change our thinking. Our hearts are no different. We wreck havoc on our precious hearts by letting anyone and everyone near them in the name of *love* before we truly explore the definition and entertain the idea of *loving* ourselves unconditionally. By first discovering self-love, we can identify love from others when it is truly present. People, God does not fail us. God gives us tools so that we can up lift ourselves to a higher place. It's been thirty days now and Lord knows we've been working. You should at least have a little muscle and some mental discipline. So

I say to you, turn not away from your Father God for He is not the one who condemns, judges, and mistreats you. He will never fail you. We fail ourselves when we reject the truth that GOD is all GOOD, and always present in our lives.

Take Home Sample Routine for Fall

Exercise: What is the one thing in your heart of hearts that you would like to be forgiven for? This is about you. Right now, no one else applies. Find a quiet and comfortable space, gather your pen and pad and sit down. Before you start writing, take three deep breaths. Inhale through your nose and exhale through your mouth. Close your eyes and think. When you have gotten your answer write it. Start off like this: Dear (your name), Today I am forgiving you for _____. God forgives you as well. Holding on to this memory no longer serves me. I no longer condemn myself. I love myself. I am forgiven, and I am free. And so it is. Read this note over and over to yourself until you believe that you are truly free from it.

Stretch: Expand your consciousness by meditating on the idea of *health*.

Day Thirty-One: Health

Health is God's original intent for mankind. The fact that our bodies experience something as common as a cold to something as fatal as cancer is all due to the erroneous belief that we must get sick. Some people believe that sickness has to be a part of life. It is evident when we say things like I get a sore throat in the winter, or I'll get cramps during my period. These things do not have to be true for you. You only believe they are true, because someone told you these things and you expected for them to happen. So they did.

Before there was any sickness, pain, or mental disturbance in the body, it was healthy first. This is because health is true. Illness is the residual effect of everything done out of truth. Before health can become evident in the body, the idea of it must take root in the mind. This is only logical if the mind controls the body. Seeking health as a state of consciousness first will only insure the optimal results as it relates to the maintenance or restoration of all bodily functions.

It never amazes me when a doctor gives people their life expectancy that the individual who focuses their heart and mind on the power of the Lord suddenly becomes healed from their *fatal* disease. Those who focus on the goodness of God not only heal themselves; they live a life that is rich and full of joy; because now they have a testimony. We can live from a place of health and wholeness now if we focus on the Greatness of God. One day, we will get to the point where we can really heal our lives. One day we will grow in the consciousness that we need not even get sick. Until then, wouldn't it be nice to walk into our doctor's office and say, *"What up doc? I'm just here for my yearly affirmation of perfect health, and vitality, and by the way since you didn't have to do much work you can keep the bill!"* I can't wait for that day. What about you?

Exercise: Deny with me: No matter what is showing up on the outside of my body right now, I am not concerned. I know my true state is perfect health, and I accept this truth with my heart and mind. No pain and sickness can bring me to my knees, because I am now standing on truth. The truth supports me. It uplifts me, and it gives me the energy and strength I deserve to live a life fulfilled. I am not sick. I am not sick; because I am not my body. I can never be sick; because I am one with God. Right here, right now I am healthy. I am whole and I am complete. As I affirm this truth, I witness the negative thoughts disguised as sickness disappear into the nothingness in which they came.

Stretch: Expand your consciousness by contemplating what it means to ***exercise***.

Day Thirty-Two: Exercise

I know that it may be difficult for some of you to make the distinction between exercise and working out because you've been using them interchangeably for so long. However, it is imperative for your spiritual development to understand that there is a fundamental difference between *exercising* and *working out*.

Exercise is the internal process by which you, the trainee, work with ideas in your mind to shape and form substance. Substance is those things that you desire to bring into your life. For example, a sculpted body is an example of substance, but you have to mentally prepare yourself first by working with the *idea* of health or beauty before that sculpted body can materialize. Only then, after the internal process of mental exercise has taken root, can you begin to workout.

Working out is the external process. Working out are all of the things that you, the trainee, do in the material or *physically* to accomplish your goals. For example, you want to lose twenty pounds and lower your cholesterol. Here is an example of an exercise regimen. Meditate on the idea of health. Then visualize in your mind what perfect health would look like to you. Write down what you see in your mind. Journal about the things you would do when you lose those twenty pounds and lower your cholesterol. Affirmatively pray about it. Thank the Holy Spirit in advance for showing you the perfect way to achieve your desired outcome. Wait patiently as the Holy Spirit reveals to you the perfect plan. When you hear your answer, write it down. Proceed as the plan is revealed to you. This is your *work out* phase!

Here is an example of the workout plan: Go to your refrigerator and freezer and clean it out entirely. Once the refrigerator and freezer are clean, restock them with only the lean cuts of poultry, fruits, vegetables, grains, and good fats. Take a garbage bag from the pantry and throw away all processed foods, red meats, trans and saturated fats and white sugar. Trash it. Prepare a salad, and baked some chicken so that after you come home from the gym, you can enjoy a delicious chicken salad. Write out your healthy meal plan and your workout regimen for the month, and follow it just as the Holy Spirit prescribed.

It is important to understand that exercise and working out go hand and hand. However, working out should not proceed the internal process of exercise, because when it does, things hardly ever go as smoothly. When we attempt to manipulate the outer before we summon the counsel of the Holy Spirit, we are looking to run into a brick wall. So, before you workout, exercise.

Exercise: Pray with me: Lord God, help me stop wasting valuable energy trying to manipulate the things that are outside of me. Thank you for showing me how to tap into the power within. Help me discipline my mind, holding on to thoughts that are only righteous and true. Thank you for teaching me how to exercise so that my workouts don't have to be so difficult. In this, I pray. Amen.

Stretch: Expand your consciousness by meditating on *food*.

Day Thirty-Three: Food

Food is for substance. In other words, it is to sustain. The appropriation of the food you digest can either sustain your health, or debilitate your health. It has always been a common practice in the medical field for the doctor to change the patient's diet as soon as the patient is admitted. Modern psychology is now linking diet to different types of mental and behavioral disorders such as ADHD, schizophrenia, and depression. We can do anything we would like to do externally, but our efforts will be in vain if we neglect our internal selves. What goes in, must come out, and this act of coming out is not only limited to a bowel movement. It can come out in your thoughts, moods, and behaviors.

When I speak of food, I not only speak of that which we put in our mouths. I am also talking about what we put in our minds. Everything that we appropriate both physically and mentally must come out. If we eat greasy foods, we are likely to have pimples and problems with our arteries. If we listen to hostile degrading music, we are likely to behave aggressively and subject ourselves to people and circumstances that degrade us. You are what you eat. So chose to eat clean.

Exercise: Affirm with me: I respect my body. Therefore, I only replenish it with the things that are going to give me the best possible outcome, both physically and mentally. I eat foods that are nutritious and healthy. I love green vegetables, colorful sweet and juicy fruits, and wholesome whole grains. I love nuts and seeds and lean white meat. I know that when I replenish my body with these foods, I will not only look stunning, I'll also feel energetic, my mood will be light and easy, and my mental eye will see things more clearly. I am ready to be rejuvenated starting from within. I love food, but I also respect the temple that God gave me, so I feed it the best foods nature has to offer and so it is!

Stretch: Expand your consciousness by reflecting on the idea of ***eating***.

Day Thirty-Four: Eating

EAT ONLY WHEN YOU ARE HUNGRY! You'll hear many different theories on eating. I have tried them all so I can only tell you what I've discovered. I've eaten three meals a day, breakfast, lunch, and dinner. I've also eaten 6-8 meals a day to sustain muscle mass and speed up my metabolism. I've also eaten one meal a day, and I've fasted for days at a time without eating anything for 24-hour periods. What I've discovered after trying all of these theories is one thing. If I feel empty inside, no matter how much I eat or how little I eat, my appetite will be ferocious. No protein diet will make me feel sustained. Nor will eating 6-8 meals a day keep me full. Our appetites reflect our level of fulfillment in our personal lives.

People eat when they are hungry. They eat when they feel they are missing something. It is not the message sent to the brain that signals the body that it needs to eat that keeps us opening the refrigerator. It is the appetite for *something more* that keeps us stuffing our faces. We try and feed a need or desire with food and we keep packing on the pounds because it simply cannot be done. If we are lonely, we pull out the Ben and Jerry's. If we are bored, we munch on chocolate chip cookies. If we are mad, we order Mexican. If we are irritable and nervous, we want chocolate. Some may call this emotional eating and that is a relevant term. However, it goes deeper than that.

Have you ever been so involved in a project or spent the day doing something you loved to do and you just forgot to eat. For some reason you just weren't hungry. All day you were so caught up in your love interest that food never crossed your mind, or pinched your stomach. Ever wonder why that happens? It happens because when you are so immersed, you are filling yourself with the most satisfying food, in which only God can provide. Remember food is not only lima beans, and sweet potatoes. Food is also thoughts, ideas and desires, and when you're sorting those things out, you are having one heck of a feast.

Now, have you ever had so much to do, and in between doing it, you kept running to the kitchen because you felt hungry, or needed to munch on something? In this case, you were probably bored although you appeared to be busy. You were probably working out of obligation. Because the passion and fulfillment was not there, you got bored and sought substance elsewhere.

When we are truly doing what we love, our energies are focused on that thing. Nothing can pull us from it. Not food, not sex, not even money. At that time, we are so engaged in our love interest that our mind and hearts are on overload and our tummies are too. The next time you *feel* like eating, ask yourself, *Am I really hungry, or am I just craving something that has a little more substance.*

Exercise: Affirm with me: I eat when I am truly hungry. I know when I am hungry, because my brain will send an unmistakable signal to my stomach that cannot be denied. When this happens, I will remain discipline and eat just enough to satisfy my physical hunger. There is no need for me to eat fast or stuff myself with large amounts, because I know that there is more than enough and there is always tomorrow. I eat for nourishment, not for entertainment. As I go about my day making sure that I indulge myself in my many fun and fulfilling projects, I become more aware that my ferocious appetite is just a figment of my imagination. And so it is.

Stretch: Expand your consciousness by reflecting on *resistance*.

Day Thirty-Five: Resistance

When it comes to resistance, less is more, contrary to popular belief. Our bodies are fashion for the best outcome without a lot of wear and tear placed upon them. Remember the body is a self renewing organism, so that means whether we tear down muscle with resistance training or not, new muscle will grow and repair itself. The use of resistance training is just to hurry things along as it relates to physical strength and muscle gain.

I used to be under the assumption that I needed to lift heavy loads of weight five to six days a week to achieve maximum results. It wasn't until recently that I decided to see what my body was capable of doing with the use of very little weight. Sometimes, I would use my own body weight or no weight at all. The results were the same, and I felt a lot better. I should also mention that because I was working with my own body weight, and concentrating more on the idea of repetition as opposed to pushing and pulling heavy dumbbells and barbells, I subjected myself to less injury, and less fatigue.

Some may say that the weight that I use is too light. I understand this. After ten years of heavy lifting, if you want to continue to max out, you really have to lift the entire gym. However, I am a fan of repetition. Instead of lifting more, I like to go the distance. By completing more reps, you not only get in more cardio training which is good for the *heart,* you also build more elastic and flexible muscle. I'm sure there is a small percentage of you reading this that wants to gain more weight. Traditionally, the advice would be to lift heavier and eat more calories. If you would like to follow this advice, that is your choice. You can, however, gain more weight if you simply consume more calories. As it relates to holistic health, that is something that I would like you to consider.

There is a Spiritual Law called the law of resistance. The Law is simple. It simply means that the more you resist something, the more the opposition builds up. The Law states that resistance is not in accordance with nature. Nature, in its natural state, does not fight to do anything. The wind does not struggle to blow, it just blows. Man, however, not understanding this law, still believes in resistance.

Anything we resist, we have to fight against. In fitness, the term resistance training is to push and pull. Pushing and pulling is fighting against. Where there is resistance, there is no surrender. Where there is no surrender, there is war.

I won't give you too much direction as to what to do as it relates to resistance training. I will however leave you with this. I believe life was designed so that you and I can live in peace and in harmony. It was not set up for us to struggle and fight. Believing in resistance is what brings about our biggest wars. In the Oxford English dictionary, resistance is described as armed or violent opposition. I also learned something that I never knew when looking up the word in the dictionary. Did you know that there was an underground movement formed in France during World War Two to fight the German occupying forces and the Vichy government that was called *THE RESISTANCE*?

Many of you believe in resistance and can't see how you can live without it. I used to hold similar beliefs. However, when I began to study truth and practice the law of non-resistance in my life, I must say battles that I could not win with all the ammunition in the world turned into effortless victories. Victory was mine by divine right.

It was easy for me to put this Law into practice at home, at work, and in relationships. I must admit that it was a challenge for me to put this law into practice at the gym. Everything I believed in was challenged. *How was I going to get into shape? How was I going to keep my thighs toned? Wasn't my metabolism going to slow down? Was I on my way to being fat again?* These are the question you ask yourself when you begin to work out before you work in. Had I built my inner strength first, I would have known that I did not have to practice resistance at all in order to get in shape. *The fact of the matter was and still is the shape was already there, and the shape will always be there, so there was no need for me to get in it. What I needed to do was accept it and do the things necessary so that I could become one with it.* This is what people like the yogis knew. This is what Buddha and Jesus knew. There is no fight to get in shape. We need not tear anything down to build it up. We need only eliminate that which is not beneficial to our well being and the shape will sculpt itself. In the natural process of elimination, everything that is not originally like you will fall away leaving behind your authentic perfectly sculpted body.

I cannot begin to tell you how many women have distorted their original design with excessive resistance training. Some of them, you cannot even recognize. I remember I looked in the mirror one night after I had taken off my shirt and bra, and I looked at my breast. Why were they moving down south? I haven't bore any children. I have no mate or child that tugs and pulls on them so why are they moving in the direction that they were? It was explained to me that flat bench pressing builds the upper pectoral muscle. While this exercise may give a man exactly what he is looking for, it does the opposite for a woman, because she has breasts. When she builds the upper pectoralis, the breasts drop. So many women resort to cosmetic surgery in the fitness industry after they have altered the original design with excessive resistance training. The attempt is to make their bodies look more feminine again. They get breast augmentation and butt implants, never entertaining the thought that maybe it was resistance that got them there in the first place.

The Law of Non-Resistance as applied to my fitness regimen is a progressive attempt for me to implement change. While I used to weight train six days a week, I have now decreased to three days or less. My weight is not heavy. Sometimes it is completely absent. There are days when I use my own body weight. I now incorporate modern exercise like core training, Pilates, yoga, and calisthenics in my routines. What I've found about these types of exercises is that they are not as modern as they seem. They have been around since ancient times, and now they are making a comeback like everything that is true seems to do. The Law of Non-Resistance is not an easy one to accept, especially if you were raised to fight for what you want. It's okay; be patient with yourself. Begin to practice non-resistance where you feel comfortable. The last thing I want you to do is resist against the Law of Non-Resistance.

Exercise: Pray with me: Father God, I come to you with the intention of living a life directed by Spirit. I understand that there are spiritual laws that govern this universe. My focus is to be in accordance with them. Some laws are easier to put into practice than others. Others require patience and subtle application. In any event, I am here willing to at least try whatever I believe will bring me closer to You. If You say I must give in order to receive, let me give joyfully that which is good. If You say success requires that I change and grow, let me except change and grow wiser with every experience. If You say I am the thinker who thinks the thought that makes the thing manifest, then I ask you to help me concentrate on the idea of love. Lord God, if You tell me that resistance produces an inevitable flow of negative energy, then I ask You to show me how to flow through life like the river. Lord God, it is my desire to do Your will, and I don't want to ever be foolish enough to resist against that. Lord God, I ask You for Your help, and I thank You for Your help. For in You, I find strength and that is something I shall not resist.

Stretch: Expand your consciousness by reflecting on **repetition**.

Day Thirty-Six: Repetition

The best way to learn something is to repeat it. When you repeat something, you not only hear it, and say it, you began to feel it. You should understand that 'thought' and 'feel' work together to materialize that which is desired. To repeat a thing with no concentration is a waste of time and energy. This is true when we speak of exercising to sculpt our bodies. It is also true when we are trying to erase negative beliefs, and form positive thoughts. Saying, "There is no evil in the world" one hundred times will not make you believe it. Nor will doing twenty five repetitions of squats to sit your buttocks up higher. Each movement has to be executed with proper form and technique, and for that to be done you make the mind-body connection.

You have to understand what you are doing. You have to believe that every repetition you complete will bring you closer to your desired goal. When prayer was first introduced to me, I didn't understand what I was doing. I learned how to say them because I had repeated them. I did not understand them because they were taught to me in Arabic first and that was not *my* original language. When they were translated in English, I had a better understanding. Now that I understood the prayer, I could decide if I believed them. The ones I believed I continued to repeat and I watched the good they brought into my life. The ones that did not agree with me, I simply discarded.

The same is true in fitness. I remember I saw my mother doing squats when I was younger. She looked happy doing them so I decided to do them on my own when I got older. Nothing significant happened except sometimes I'd get stiff and sore, but there were no changes in my anatomy that I could see. I read a fitness magazine that told me what squats were for, and that I had to eat a certain way to see the fruits of my labor. Once I incorporated the knowledge and the diet into my daily routine, I began to see the results. Now I believe in this exercise. Repetition will always heat the water. Thought and feeling will bring it to a boil. Once you add understanding and belief in the pot, you've got yourself a meal.

Exercise: Affirm with me: In my mind I repeatedly play thoughts that I wish to see in my world and affairs. From my mouth, I only repeat words that uplift and empower. When I exercise, I understand that I must concentrate on the movement so that the repetition will work. I use the power of repetition wisely.

Stretch: Expand your consciousness by meditating on **endurance**.

Day Thirty-Seven: Endurance

You hear some fitness professionals use the term *endurance training* rather than resistance training. Since I have come into this consciousness, I use the term endurance training as well. What they both have in common is that they increase strength. The difference however is how strength is acquired. One requires friction; the other does not. To endure is to stand, experience, sustain, last, continue, persist, and tolerate. You are still getting the job done, but without the friction and without force. There is no pushing against, or pulling from, when you are practicing endurance. Examples of endurance training are stretching, isometrics, and various forms of cardio. Instead of tearing down the muscle, you are stretching it, making it more elastic, and pliable. When you do this, you are still taking your body out of its comfort zone, so you are still testing your limits. Because the muscle is more flexible, it is better suited to endure more. The same principle applies to your consciousness. You expand it so that you are not narrow-minded. When the consciousness is expanded, you can take in and process more information. This process of expansion gives you a better quality of life--making it so that you can produce more.

Too much resistance training and no flexibility leaves the body prone to all types of aliments. In fact, it can do more harm than good. Many weight lifters and fitness competitors have experienced injuries such as torn rotator cuffs, fractured spinal columns and herniated disks. I once saw a man blow out his knee doing squats, all this because they failed to practice a little endurance.

Think about this--you can do *resistance training* and tone and sculpt muscle, or you can practice *endurance training* and tone and sculpt muscle, become more flexible, and build strength. Now that's maximizing your potential. With endurance, the only thing that can stop you from reaching your goal is the lack of mental stamina. This shouldn't be a problem since we are learning how to focus our thoughts.

It's only logical to practice endurance because it's a natural state and it provides the same benefits with fewer struggles.

Exercise: Pray with me: Lord God, I endure all that is good in Your name.

Stretch: Expand your consciousness by reflecting on what it means to have ***stamina***.

Day Thirty-Eight: Stamina

The dictionary describes stamina as the ability to sustain prolonged physical or mental effort. It is safe to say then that no one can achieve victory without having stamina. In order for the athlete to achieve his gold medal, stamina must be present. If the college graduate wants to receive his degree, stamina has to be applied during his studies. If the metaphysician wants to create the life that he wants to live, immense stamina must be applied to his way of thinking. You need stamina too. Every client that I've trained that has met their fitness goals had to have stamina. If you are serious about making health and fitness a way of life for you, you too will need stamina.

Exercise: For fun, let's test our stamina. Get into squat position. Spread your feet shoulder width apart. Bend your knees until you feel as if you're sitting on an invisible chair. Keep your back straight, shoulders square, and your chin up. Place your hands wherever feels most comfortable. You can put them on your hips, at your sides, or you can hold them out in front of you. Just hold that position. If you want to, you can count to yourself. This will let you know how long you were able to sustain that position, so the next time you try it again you can have something to measure. Stop whenever you want. This is your own personal test. Just so you know, that was endurance training. We call that exercise isometric training, what you were measuring however was your stamina.

Affirm with me: My stamina helps me make one demonstration after the other.

Stretch: Expand your consciousness by meditating on the word ***definition***.

Day Thirty-Nine: Definition

On rare occasions I get a client who comes to me and says, *"Look, I don't want to lose any weight. I just want a little more definition."* I always smile at this type. What I'm hearing is that they've already done the ground work; in fitness we call this conditioning. They are telling me I've already gotten rid of the baggage. I already have the shape I want. All I want to do now is build more *character.* What I hear is, I want to study further. My desire is to improve.

I have fun with and I learn from all of my clients but the ones that want to define are the ones I usually end up exercising with from time to time. Because they are already conditioned, have endurance, and stamina, they don't slow me down. If there is an exercise that I am doing that she does not recognize, she can watch me and catch on quickly. If I should stop to show her the technique, it doesn't intercept my flow because she is a fast learner.

Definition, in this case is just fine tuning, showing the way, giving direction, and touching up. Have you ever had to prepare for a test, and all you had to do was look over your notes because you thoroughly studied the chapters previously? That's defining. In fitness, we help a client define their physique by tweaking their nutrition, and incorporating more repetition within their sets. In life, we define ourselves with words and thoughts for these things carve out our experiences.

When the sessions are up for the client who wanted more definition, she usually asks for me to jot down a nutrition plan and a regimen that she can refer back to on her own whenever she needs refreshing. Sometimes, she just remembers what has been taught and she makes up her own routines and puts together her own meal plan. When I see her weeks and months later, she is indeed more defined than when we departed.

There are some who come to me and appear to be defined, as a matter of fact, they are ripped. But as I train them as I would a conditioned athlete, I uncover that their master piece was built on a shaky foundation. While their bodies are toned and shapely, something else is missing. Perhaps they acquired that shape falsely using chemicals and crash diets. Perhaps they had cosmetic surgery. If they make no mention of it, neither do I. What I know is that they need to be *conditioned* again. Not only do they need to be conditioned again, they need to build *endurance* and *stamina*. These defined clients are the hardest to train because they are stuck in a self-debilitating condition. They've been looking in the mirror at what appears to be perfection, so they cannot perceive rebuilding what their work of art. I enjoy training this person as much as I enjoy training the truly conditioned athlete. First of all, it is a challenge for me, and second it reminds me that the journey is always more important than the destination.

Exercise: Affirm with me: I define myself by the standards of God.

Stretch: Expand your consciousness with the word **muscle**.

Day Forty: Muscle

I love muscle. Muscle represents physical power. My love for muscle is what kept me believing in the need to hold on to that which was no longer a part of me. My love of muscle almost enslaved me. It had me carrying around and holding up other peoples' opinions and beliefs about me and who I should be. Muscle had me thinking I needed to push and pull my way through life in order to be recognized and respected. The more muscle I built, the more I was ready to fight. Then one day I found myself swinging like a mad woman in thin air. I felt someone tapped me on the shoulder. I turned around and found myself surrounded by the blue sea. Although I could see no one, I knew someone was there.

"You can stop fighting now," she said. With that, I tied my denim jacket around my waist and took a seat on the warm sand.

"It is obvious that you are strong. You need not prove that. God generously gives strength to us all and you are no exception." And then I felt soft fingers squeeze my bicep.

"My, you've worked so hard for so long. Why don't you take some time off and let someone else do the work? Wouldn't that be nice?" She sounded as if she was trying to coerce me. Besides, what did she know about me? Furthermore, how would she handle my business if I wasn't there? She'd just screw things up.

"Wouldn't you enjoy some time to rest both your body and your mind so that your heart can be healed and your energy restored?" Now she was getting to me. Anytime someone starts to talk about my heart, I get a little sensitive. I wanted to shout yes, but for some reason I could not talk.

"For goodness sake, Nadirah look at you. You're too beautiful to be so angry. You're too intelligent to act so foolishly. I know you're strong, but I would still like to at least help. I usually don't say this, but I insist." That got me. I could use the time off. She didn't show a resume but for some reason I felt she was suited for the job.

Nothing is wrong with building muscle if that's what you want to do. There is, however, something wrong if you are building the muscle with the intent to fight. I didn't realize I was building muscle because I had a belief in fighting; but after Spirit took over it gave me time for introspection. I began to search my subconscious and I found things that were buried all the way back to my childhood. I searched and search, tracing back my childhood all the way up to the beach where Spirit took over. I must admit, she knew something because she was right. All this time, I believed that I needed to fight and my obsession with resistance training and building muscle supported that.

Every day I trained, I was preparing for war like a soldier. With no weapon in hand, my mind would suffice. I was my toughest adversary. I tussled with my own self. Every fight brought me to my knees. I struggled against feeling angry. I fought against the thought of being poor. I balled up my fist and punched down the walls that discriminated against me because I was a *black woman*. I pushed down the urges of my vagina after abstaining for so long that I screamed for it to shut up. I clutched my heart when it started to beat fast because I didn't want others to hear my fear. I *held* up my reputation for the sake of my family and my religious community. I packed my body up and kept it so tight for the fellahs, nearly cutting off my circulation. I quietly stomped around in life, because I did not want to *feel*. My feelings scared me. I had no safe place to put them, so I tried to *work them out of me*. Like many who *work out*, I became exhausted. I hadn't gotten to the root, so things kept falling apart. I needed to work *in*, but how? I wanted to go away but where would I go? Nowhere. I would go nowhere but inside of myself, and feel what I was feeling; and I would do nothing about it.

That's right, I needed to practice non-resistance. I could feel my emotions, and not attack myself or anyone else. Pushing them down and cutting them off only made them grow stronger. As each emotion rose up, I sat quietly. I breathed deeply, and I said, "I acknowledge your presence. What can I do for you?" Some days were harder than others; because some days, I could not get to the root. As you might imagine for a person who has been practicing resistance training, it would be easy to resist. I could not do that. So I sat. Some days, I laid on my back. Some days, I wrote in my journal. Some days, I lit a candle and just stared at it for hours until the wax turned into hot fluid and ran off my desk. Most days, I prayed. Some days, I was too mad and ashamed to pray, but when I did, it was short and sweet. "Lord God, why am I feeling this way? Please show me why." Some days, He was slow in His reply. Perhaps, I was still impatient. In any event, you can't rush Spirit. So I waited. Then She spoke. "Every feeling is a signal to let you know if what you're doing is in alignment with what I have planned for your life. My child, I only want you to feel good. If you are feeling bad, we need to make some adjustments."

For forty days, I explored my feelings. I made adjustments where they were needed. I am still not done. Every day I sat, God showed me some new work that He has cut out for me. The funny thing about it, what was presented as work looked like recreation to me. I intend to pursue it wholeheartedly because I love the Lord, and I am so grateful to Spirit for rescuing me from myself. Any work that I do for Him shall be done in love because He showed me love when He helped me build *spiritual muscle*, and promised me that I'd never have to fight again.

Exercise: There is no exercise for today. I'm allowing you to rest. You've earned it. I would like for you to stretch.

Stretch: Expand your consciousness by concentrating on the **love of GOD**.

Bibliography

- Spiritual Laws for each Season are from Raymond Holliwell's book, *Working with the Law*
- Affirmations and Denials for each season are from H. Emilie Cady's *Lessons in Truth*
- Deeper Insights for some of the words used in the book are from Charles Fillmore's *The Revealing Word*
- Some words are defined in detail using Webster's and Oxford's Dictionary

About the Author

For the past twelve years I served my community as a certified holoistc fitness practitioner, personal trainer, fitness conselor, group ex-cordinator, and am currently a student of Universal Law and Christian Metaphysics.

While working as a fitness practitioner I've had to work through my own mental, emotional, and spiritual baggage in order to acheieve my own fitness goals and make peace with my body.

I live in Miami Gardens Florida with my family Vicki, Fatih, Aaliyah, Zakiyyah, and Jihad Shakir. I am still serving my community as a Fitness manager, and a holistic fitness practitioner. Visit me anytime at www.NadirahAqueelahShakir.com.